Lunchtime Enlightenment

Meditations to Transform Your Life <u>Now</u>—
at Work, at Home, at Play

PRAGITO DOVE

PENGUIN COMPASS

PENGUIN COMPASS
Published by the Penguin Group
Penguin Putnam Inc., 375 Hudson Street,
New York, New York 10014, U.S.A.
Penguin Books Ltd, 80 Strand, London WC2R 0RL, England
Penguin Books Australia Ltd, 250 Camberwell Road,
Camberwell, Victoria 3124, Australia
Penguin Books Canada Ltd, 10 Alcorn Avenue,
Toronto, Ontario, Canada M4V 3B2
Penguin Books India (P) Ltd, 11 Community Centre,
Panchsheel Park, New Delhi - 110 017, India
Penguin Books (N.Z.) Ltd, Cnr Rosedale and Airborne Roads,
Albany, Auckland, New Zealand
Penguin Books (South Africa) (Pty) Ltd, 24 Sturdee Avenue,
Rosebank, Johannesburg 2196, South Africa

Penguin Books Ltd, Registered Offices:
Harmondsworth, Middlesex, England

First published in the United States of America by Viking Compass 2001
Published in Penguin Compass 2002

1 3 5 7 9 10 8 6 4 2

Copyright © Pragito Dove, 2001
All rights reserved

PUBLISHER'S NOTE
This is a reference book not intended to treat, diagnose, or prescribe. The
information contained herein is in no way to be considered as a substitution
for a consultation with a duly licensed health care professional.

THE LIBRARY OF CONGRESS HAS CATALOGED THE HARDCOVER EDITION AS FOLLOWS:
Dove, Pragito.
Lunchtime enlightenment: modern meditations to free the mind and
unleash the spirit at work, at home, at play / Pragito Dove.
p.   cm.
ISBN 0-670-89457-5 (hc.)
ISBN 0 14 21.9605 3 (pbk.)
1. Meditation.   2. Osho, 1931–1990.   I. Title.
BP605.R342 D68 2001
299'.93—dc21   2001017745

Printed in the United States of America
Set in Bembo
Designed by Susan Hood

PENGUIN
COMPASS

LUNCHTIME ENLIGHTENMENT

Pragito Dove has twenty years' experience as a consultant and trainer in stress management, relaxation, meditation, and meditation counseling. Since 1988 she has worked with executives and employees at Bay Area corporations, including the *San Francisco Chronicle* and Autodesk. For several years she has lead a highly successful and popular "Lunchtime Enlightenment" meditation series at Stacey's Bookstore in San Francisco's financial district, which became the inspiration for this book. She lives in Marin County, California.

To Osho

ACKNOWLEDGMENTS

There are many people who have given their support in the writing of this book. No one writes a book alone and there are many whom I wish to thank for their contribution to me personally and to the book.

I can't imagine having a better editor than Janet Goldstein at Viking Penguin. I have truly enjoyed her creative ideas, practical know-how, enthusiasm, and support for this project from the get-go.

To Tom Grady, a great agent who has guided me through the maze of the publishing world with such care, using his skills and experience to make the whole process flow with grace and ease.

To Brenda Rosen for her considerable help in developing the proposal for this book.

To my wonderful structural editor, Caroline Pincus. Your warmth, humor, and creativity have truly made working with you the greatest pleasure.

Thank you to Osho International for allowing me to enrich the text with a selection of Osho's meditation techniques from the book *Meditation—The First and Last Freedom*.

A special thank you to Colleen Lindsay, for your insight and vision for first inviting me to do the series at Stacey's. And Ann Trinca, for your enthusiasm and hard work and for first naming the Stacey's series "Lunchtime Enlightenment." And Calla Devlin, Ingrid Nystrom, Jim Breeden, and all the staff at Stacey's for making my series there such an enjoyable affair. I was always greeted with such warmth, affection, and respect.

To Karen West and Jen Pfeiffer at the Barnes & Noble stores—your insight and interest.

All the wonderful women at the San Francisco chapter of NAWBO (National Association of Women Business Owners); the Charter 100 Club, San Francisco chapter; and MAFE (the Marin branch of the National Association of Female Executives) for your warmth, enthusiam, humor, and invaluable support of my work.

From a deep place in my heart I would like to thank all the people whose stories in this book have served us all so well.

I cannot thank you enough, Manuela Dunn. You have been a constant source of support and friendship, sharing with me your expertise and knowledge of the publishing world.

To the following friends who have lent wisdom and encouragement in my work and life: Mary O'Connor, Carol Oakes, and Helen Strodl.

Jeanette Vonier for being an outstanding photographer and friend.

Betsy Bliss Nicholls for your ideas and input into the manuscript.

A very special thank you to Aileen Harvey who read the book in manuscript and added the wisdom of her heart and mind.

To Nirvan Richard Santoro my longtime accountant and friend—thank you for guiding me through the intricacies of the financial world with such loving care.

To Yogi Douglas Matheson, over many, many years I have appreciated your generous friendship.

Ricardo Molczadzki—the best acupuncturist in the world—thank you for your wisdom, insight, and compassionate heart.

Niranjan Evarts for your generous support, friendship, and creative ideas.

Rahasya Barrack—your constant love and encouragement are a treasure that I cherish.

My dear friend Paula Zand. You are a very special person whose wisdom, love, and friendship are invaluable to me. Thank you for helping me find my own courage and for being there. What a gift you are to this world.

And last, but certainly not least, to my son Paul. Thank you for believing in me, for your love and support, for your wonderful sense of humor, your authenticity, wisdom, and intelligence. You're the greatest.

CONTENTS

Introduction

My day is probably a lot like yours, full of tasks and details, errands and deadlines, decisions and emotions. I have found that by incorporating a few simple meditation techniques into my daily routine, everything I do goes more smoothly, and life proceeds at a more relaxed rhythm and with much less stress.

Today, for instance, because my mind feels particularly scattered and busy, I begin the day with a meditation practice in which I sit and hum for forty-five minutes and then lie down in silence for fifteen minutes. After I shower and dress, I prepare the room slowly and carefully by tidying up, arranging a comfortable cushion, and putting on the music soundtrack that I use to accompany this technique. Then I sit down with my back straight, yet relaxed. As soon as I do, I begin to feel my inner strength, a calm dignity that pervades my whole being. It's as if my body knows that this posture invites a wonderfully peaceful state. I close my eyes and begin to hum along with the music, keeping my mouth open as I hum.

As the sound vibrations fill my body, the chatter in my mind starts to quiet down. With the mind more calm, I am able to tap into feelings of sadness about the recent death of my father, allowing my emotions to emerge as the healing vibration of the humming envelops me in a cocoon of love and comfort. When thoughts about a difficult business contract trigger feelings of anger, I continue to hum as the energy of anger rises, pushing it out through my open mouth. The anger washes over me like a tidal wave, and then just as quickly it is gone, replaced by a feeling of confidence in my ability to find a creative solution to the problem. I notice my sense of humor returning.

When the music stops, I lie down on the carpet in silence, keeping my eyes closed. The energy created by the humming reaches every corner of my being. I feel the floor underneath me support my whole body, and I sink into a deep sense of trust in myself and the universe. When a chime sounds after fifteen minutes, I slowly come to a sitting position. I don't hurry but rather move deliberately, feeling calmly active and looking forward to the possibilities the new day holds.

Beginning the day with a meditation technique brings a quality of relaxed awareness and presence to everything I do. I savor the aroma and flavor of my cup of breakfast tea, feed the cat, then straighten up the kitchen and take out the trash slowly and mindfully. Some years ago when I was still taking my son to school in the mornings, I learned to create a rhythm for him by establishing a routine that I continue for myself to this day.

Rhythm has a calming effect on the body and mind. It soothes and nourishes our heart and soul. Over the years I have noticed that I have come to talk more slowly and carefully. Remembering to breathe with awareness before I speak helps, especially in a crisis. It reminds me to come down from the head into the body. And staying connected with the body helps me stay connected to myself. When my now grown-up son calls this morning in a panic because he has lost his passport, my relaxed response calms him, and we are quickly able to come up with a solution.

As my day proceeds, I continue to use meditation to keep me focused, yet relaxed. At lunchtime, I eat slowly and with awareness, enjoying each texture and taste. The phone is turned off, and I don't read. Because it's a cool and sunny fall day, I take a walk after lunch to give my body a break from the tension of work. Although the mind speaks to us with words, the body uses feelings, which can be expressed both as physical sensations and emotions. Meditation has taught me to listen to my body, noticing when it sends signals of stress and tension so that I can bring it back into balance before it sends the stronger signal of pain.

At the end of the workday, I do an active meditation technique to free the body from physical tensions and the mind from any emotional or mental stress that has built up. Since I have spent most of today sitting at my desk staring at the computer screen, I release the physical tension that has accumulated by dancing for forty-five minutes to a special music soundtrack with my eyes closed and then lying down in silence for fifteen minutes.

My days are not perfect or stressless, but my meditation practice gives me abundant tools for bringing awareness as I move through my day.

On this particular day I had plenty of time for longer meditations because I was working at home. Not all my days are like this. I often see many clients in a day or drive to downtown San Francisco to teach meditation classes as a consultant to large corporations. I also travel around the state and sometimes out of state to facilitate workshops. Some days, and weeks, are a lot more stressful than others, especially when I am working on a deadline or find complications arising in my schedule.

I practice (and teach) a range of techniques—some that take just a few minutes, others that take an hour or more. The shorter techniques keep me going at the airport, in traffic, in between appointments, or just when I'm having a particularly busy day. I do the longer techniques whenever I can make the time, at the beginnning or end of the day; they help to sustain me through the days when the short techniques are all I have time for. My lifestyle, probably like yours, requires careful planning *and* the ability to be adaptable to change. And so this *range* of techniques is invaluable. It affords me the luxury of having meditation in my life every day, and keeping my business of consulting, private sessions, teaching meditation workshops and trainings running efficiently.

You can have this, too.

Meditation is about paying attention. It's that simple. It is about living in the here and now instead of missing out while your mind is off making other plans.

Perhaps you associate meditation with church, sermons, dogma, or with unfamiliar Eastern beliefs. I hope that this book will dispel any misunderstandings you might have. My purpose in writing it is to show that meditation is an uncomplicated way to link the sacred with our day-to-day existence. It's for all of us. There are as many ways to meditate as you can imagine. You don't have to sit in uncomfortable positions or run off to a monastery. You don't have to meditate for over an hour a day—just ten minutes to start will be plenty. You don't have to leave your job or eliminate all stress or change your diet or your choice in clothes (though you may choose to do any one of these things). Meditation can easily be incorporated into a busy corporate office day, in commuter time, in home and family life.

Through the meditation techniques I teach in this book, you will learn to pay attention to your body, to that headache that's starting behind your eyes, to that gut feeling to take the early train home. With regular practice you will come to notice the flowers and the trees on your way to work. Meditation will change the whole quality of your day.

The book covers a range of meditation and relaxation techniques that I have learned and taught over the last twenty-two years. They follow not one tradition, but draw on all traditions I have studied, Eastern and Western, and I present them here in the hopes of inspiring you to experiment, to find the practices that work best for you.

After all, what makes life valuable and precious? It's the level of awareness that we bring to any given moment, wherever we are, whomever we are with. Too often we compartmentalize our lives, assuming that work always means stress and vacations are our only chance for relaxation. Yet we can learn to experience a relaxed alertness during every activity. Relaxed alertness gives you the luxury of being completely present and attentive and, at the same time, totally relaxed. A regular practice of meditation can teach you this quality. You will notice that staying present while talking on the phone or while driving a car in heavy traffic means you won't find your shoulders up around your ears, and that you can be relaxed and fully engaged. It does not mean that you'll be half-asleep or spaced out.

People have been meditating for thousands of years. Twenty-five centuries ago, the Buddha taught a simple technique of sitting and watching the breath that is still used to this day. Times have changed, however. No longer do we live a simple life connected to the land and to the rhythms of nature, as the Buddha did.

In ancient India, it was easy for people to sit in silence. Their pace of life was in tune with the rhythm of the earth, so they were naturally more meditative. But a meditative state often seems incompatible with contemporary life, with its physical, mental, and emotional pressures. In this book I hope to show you how to reap the benefits of meditative silence in the midst of your busy days. I will show you how meditation can help you recover your natural rhythm, your inner wisdom, and your intuition.

My Story

I know from personal experience that these techniques work. Twenty-one years ago, when my son Paul was born, I was a serious, uptight Englishwoman. Looking into my child's smiling blue eyes and seeing his innocence, trust, and joy was an incredible mirror. What had happened to those qualities in myself? I wondered. I had no trust. I lived in fear and reaction and was far too busy worrying about the future to take time to enjoy the present moment. Life was about going from one problem to the next with some temporary respite in between. On the surface I seemed happy and content. I lived in a roomy Victorian house in Saint Albans, Hertfordshire, England, with my husband and son and enjoyed a comfortable lifestyle. My work as a high school teacher of Spanish and French was rewarding. My life was "perfect." Yet inside, I was not at peace.

Looking back, it seems obvious that the chronic back pain I suffered during those years was a symptom of stress. I remember one cold and rainy November day when my back was aching more than usual, which always made me crabby and short-tempered. On the best of days, I found the Frenchwoman who was the head of my department irritating, but she had chosen this particular day to talk to me about altering my schedule, which I suspected was to suit her, rather than me. I told her in no uncertain terms that I wasn't interested in having my schedule changed. Feeling upset and inflexible, I was unwilling to make the effort to meet her halfway.

After our meeting, I faced my most difficult class, thirty-two fourteen-year-olds, most of them taking French because they had to, not because they had any interest in the language. That day they were especially restless, and my patience was shot. Toward the end of class, I launched into an authoritative speech, laying down the law about behavior, grades, attitude.

When the bell rang, I gathered up my pile of books to make a sweeping, theatrical exit from the classroom. Unfortunately the pile was off balance, and as I reached the doorway, the books slithered out of my arms and fell to the ground with a resounding crash. The class erupted in laughter. I felt stupid, ridiculous, and angry—mostly with myself. I knew very well that my students always responded better to encouragement, humor, and kindness than to stern pronouncements. I also realized with chagrin that my boss had been trying to work something out with me, and that I had been stubbornly unable to see any perspective other than my own. I was the one who was out of balance. Unless I found a way to relax, my tension and anxiety would lead to many such days.

My personal search for answers led me to discover the meditations that I now teach and that I have included in this book. I read a book on meditation and experimented at a school in London that taught the techniques of an enlightened mystic named Osho. Osho lived in a meditation resort in India where daily meditations and healing therapy workshops were (and still are) held. Osho updated many ancient meditations from a wide range of traditions and created new ones to suit today's lifestyle and psychology. I started with just ten minutes a day because an hour a day felt too overwhelming. Encouraged by the results, I tried some of Osho's longer meditations. As I experimented, I felt a tremendous release of tension. I became more calm and grounded, more relaxed about myself. Best of all, I found that I was lighter, more humorous and sincere with everyone I knew.

When my son was still quite young, I took him with me to India to visit Osho's meditation resort. As my marriage had by this time ended, the visit felt timely. Sitting with Osho in person while he gave his morning discourses, I was overwhelmed by sheer relief that I had finally found my inner "home," my connection with myself. His meditations gave me the bridge over which I could travel from fear to trust, anxiety to relaxation, low self-esteem to self-acceptance. To learn to love and respect myself and to believe that others can also love and respect me has been my greatest challenge. I ended up staying for a year on that first visit and it was there that I received my name, "Pragito," from Osho. It is a Sanskrit word and means "song." Many visits later, I trained to teach the meditations to others.

Meditation has added color, richness, and texture to the fabric of my everyday life. The changes have not been loud or dramatic, like a Wagnerian opera with thunderbolts and lightning and stunning visual effects. Rather they have crept up on me in a quiet, subtle way.

After many years and many hours of meditation practice, I found myself working as a substitute teacher for one semester in a California high school. As you can no doubt imagine, substitute teaching is not an easy job. One morning, early in my stint as a substitute, several students started making fun of my British accent when I was taking roll.

I put down the attendance book and, with a smile, started telling them a little about myself and about what it was like to teach school in England. We joked together about the differences in accent and vocabulary between the United Kingdom and the United States.

By this time in my study of meditation, I had done "The Mystic Rose Meditation" about ten times, which means that I had spent over two hundred hours laughing. (You'll find instructions for this meditation later in the book.) With all that practice, I had learned to laugh at myself easily and to use humor to lighten up potentially tense situations. As the class settled down and got to work on the day's lesson, I noticed with satisfaction how much more patient and tolerant I had become, how much less reactive, how hard it was to make me lose my cool. I trusted that my ability to create a good-humored rapport with students would bring positive results, and so it did.

The point is not that I'm the perfect meditator or perfectly healed, but neither am I the person I once was. I've been teaching meditation in India, Europe, and the United States for many years now. I currently have a practice of one-on-one sessions, hypnotherapy, stress management, and couples counseling. I also give classes, trainings, and workshops and do consulting for businesses and corporations. Meditation is an ongoing process, and the techniques and their benefits I now teach continue to be an integral part of my own personal growth.

In 1998 I was invited to give a noon-hour presentation of simple meditation practices at Stacey's Bookstore on Market Street in San Francisco's financial district. At first, I was skeptical. I had been giving only evening presentations and never before to an audience on San Francisco's "Wall Street." Wouldn't businesspeople be too busy, too preoccupied to make time in the middle of the day for meditation?

As I walked toward Stacey's on that September day amidst the hubbub of hurrying people in their smart suits and elegant shoes, my doubts grew. The word "meditation" on the sign

Stacey's had set out on the sidewalk announcing my presentation seemed absurdly out of place.

Yet when I walked into the bookstore and up the stairs, I found about two dozen well-dressed men and women waiting expectantly in the presentation area for me to begin. That first time, I led the group through a guided relaxation for the body and taught them the thirty-second stop technique (page 74) and a five-minute relax the breathing technique (page 30). By the end of the hour, their tense and serious faces were smiling and refreshed.

During the question-and-answer session at the end of the presentation, a woman lawyer asked, "How can I stop my mind? It kept chattering the whole time." I explained that the point of meditation is not to stop the mind, but simply to watch it. When we just watch, letting our thoughts pass by without judging them as good or bad, they slowly, slowly lose their power to grip us, and we get more and more in touch with our bodies and our emotions. Trying to stop the mind, I told her, just creates more tension.

A wiry young man from a financial firm asked, "Do I have to shut my eyes to meditate?" No, I told him. It's fine to meditate with your eyes open. Shutting your eyes just makes meditation easier when you're learning. It gives you a break from the workaday world and helps you direct your energy inward so that you can recharge your batteries.

The last question that day, from a harried-looking, middle-aged stockbroker, capped the event. Without a trace of humor, he asked, "How can I remember to breathe?" When the laughter died down, I suggested that he program his computer to remind him every hour, on the hour, to take a deep breath down into the belly. Or he could put a sign on his desk that read, "Remember to breathe!"

Because of the success of the first event, the store invited me back to lead monthly sessions. On the second visit, I discovered that they had given the series a name, Lunchtime Enlightenment. Those two words encapsulated the essence of what I want to teach: that the sacred and the mundane, although seemingly contradictory, are not. The key to bringing the sacred into the midst of our ordinariness is meditation.

As the lunchtime series continued, it began to take on a life of its own. I had many regulars, but there were always several newcomers. Even the first-timers seemed to fall quickly into the bubble of collective silence and profound relaxation that enveloped all present, including myself. As the months went by, the anxious questions participants had asked in the early months just fell away, and our sessions would routinely end with a deep and relaxed quiet.

What's to Come

The meditations I teach in this book are like mini-vacations you can treat yourself to anywhere at any time. Anyone can do them. No experience is needed. Whatever your goal—less stress, lower blood pressure, more creativity and flexibility, improved mental clarity or memory, a reconnection to the simple pleasure of everyday activities, even greater on-the-job productivity—meditation can help.

Here's what you will find in the pages that follow:

Part 1 defines meditation and gets you started.
Part 2 introduces you to a wide range of modern, and some ancient meditation techniques and practices that you can

use to free your mind and unleash your spirit, at work, at home, and at play.

Part 3 offers suggestions for creating your own practice and discusses the obstacles you may encounter as you develop your own style of meditating. It also covers the questions most frequently asked at my classes and workshops and reveals my top fifteen secrets for successful meditating.

A woman who came to one of my bookstore presentations told me how surprised she was to learn that there were different meditations for different kinds of stress. For instance, the Shaking, Jogging, and Working Out meditations are great for releasing physical stress, so that you can relax more easily into sitting in silence. Another great physical stress releaser, the Dancing meditation, puts you in touch with your playfulness and creativity. The Gibberish, Osho Dynamic, and Laughing meditations help release physical and mental stress, including anger and frustration, and create the inner spaciousness in which new awareness can grow. The Eating meditation, to mention just one example, can bring such awareness to your eating habits. When you are feeling emotionally upset, the Humming meditation helps heal the heart and balance the emotions.

The wide range of meditation techniques shows that meditation can be a thoroughly enjoyable way of getting an inner and outer workout, one that honors together the body, mind, and spirit. Try out several techniques and choose those that work for you, those that make you feel wonderful.

You may find that you already "know" the information contained in this book. Your inner wisdom has just been buried by work, commuting, dirty laundry, child-care arrangements, and cat-to-the-vet trips. I wrote *Lunchtime Enlightenment* to give you a range of tools and techniques that can help you reconnect to that wisdom by allowing you to get out from under the burdens we all carry as we hurtle through our fast-paced lives. The simple, modern meditations in this book can help you transform tension into creativity and dissolve your tear-out-your-hair desperation in the calm pool of peace we all have within us.

I suggest that you read the book slowly, giving yourself time to absorb and try out the different meditations. These meditations can be done alone, or in a group. It is purely a matter of personal preference. Some of you may prefer to use this book in conjunction with a meditation class or to start your own class. We each have to discover for ourselves which meditation techniques we enjoy and where and when to practice them.

Finally, a Few Words About Sitting Postures

Many of the techniques in this book do not involve sitting, but some do. For the sitting meditations, never force a posture. If you're not comfortable, any practice will simply create more tension and nothing will be achieved. If you can sit, good, but if it is a strain, try some other positions. If you cannot sit on the ground, then sit on a chair. Meditation is not afraid of chairs.

You want to take some care, of course, but don't worry too much whether your spine is absolutely erect or not. It is easy to become preoccupied with these minor things. Understand what a posture should look like and try to absorb that, then continue on your way. The essential thing is that you are comfortable and feel right.

For the sitting positions, you always want your hips to be higher than your knees to keep the stress off your back. Try placing a cushion under the hips to raise them up. You don't have to sit ramrod straight; this will make you tense. Sitting comfortably for meditation gives you a chance to get in touch with how much you like yourself. You just want to feel that your back and head are upright and in alignment, showing a sense of integrity and dignity.

May this book encourage you to find the compassion and creativity that shine within you. May it bring you peace, calmness, and relaxation.

Part One

THE BASICS

Why Meditate?

The easiest way to answer the question "Why meditate?" is to invite you to try something I do at the beginning of every new meditation class. Here's what you do:

Stand up. Now sit down again.

Now take a deep breath down into the belly and stand up again. While standing, take another deep breath, and then sit down again.

Did you notice a difference between the first and the second times? Were you more aware of what you were doing the second time? Were you more relaxed, more graceful, perhaps?

The point here is that we can bring meditative awareness and relaxation to any action, even something so ordinary as standing up and sitting down. Meditation can be as simple as breathing, the breath being the bridge between mind and body. Anytime we consciously take a breath, we move from the head down into the body and come more fully into the present moment and into relaxed awareness. It is this mind/body balance that transforms an action into a meditation.

We all have deeply embedded patterns of behavior that we act on unconsciously. We tense when the telephone rings, eat without tasting our food, or jog through the park while our mind is back in the office replaying the conversation we had with our boss or coworker. Meditation is a way of bringing these habitual behaviors to consciousness so that we can, if it's appropriate, gently release them. It helps us relax into our bodies more fully so that we are more aware of what we do and how we feel while we're doing it.

The techniques of meditation are not the invention of any one person or one school. Observers of the human condition in many different places and times have come to the conclusion that people have greater potential for conscious awareness than they generally use. Methods were developed early in India, in the fifth to twelfth century in the Syrian and Jordanian deserts, in tenth-century Japan, in medieval European monasteries, in Poland and Russia in the eighteenth and nineteenth centuries, again in India in the twentieth century, and at other times and places.

Whatever method you choose—and in this book, you will learn many—meditation is a way of getting quiet so that you can notice what's happening inside. If a man wants to break out of prison, he first has to study the layout and routine within the prison so that he can see how he might break free. To break free from stress and the other patterns of behavior that lead to unhappiness, you must first get to know how you function. Then insights and understandings will arise, and a gateway to freedom will open up.

Unless you are looking for it, you may not notice how many people have already discovered the benefits of meditation. I remember watching Arthur Ashe, many years ago, playing the match that won him the most coveted trophy in the tennis world, Wimbledon. At each net change, Ashe sat with his eyes closed for a few moments, using a meditation technique to calm and center himself. I was particularly impressed that he was willing to do this in front of so many people, undisturbed by the TV cameras trained on him and all the hoopla around him. This takes courage, especially in the high-pressure world of men's tennis. Ashe's inner game that year was particularly brilliant. Meditation helped him stay calm and centered, clear-headed, and emotionally grounded. There were no tantrums when a ruling didn't go his way, nor any victory jigs when they did. He simply played well, focused and within himself. As a keen tennis player myself, I know in a small way what Ashe experienced.

More recently, I've watched Michelle Kwan, Olympic silver medalist and two-time World Champion figure skater. Before Michelle glides onto the ice, she tries to find an empty room where she can sit quietly, eyes closed, breathing and connecting with herself. Her performances are always stunning. It is not just that Michelle has outstanding technique and athletic abil-ity, but she also displays a grace that is indefinable, as if her body and soul were responding to the music as one. She puts her whole heart into what she is doing. That quality of inte-gration, of being fully and joyfully present, is meditation in action.

Although it's not a benefit the Buddha or any other classical meditation teacher might have pointed to, meditation can also help us be more productive at work. A few years ago, the *San Jose Mercury News* ran a story about a Silicon Valley business-man named Vic Baldwin who spent nearly two hours a week meditating with his employees. The story went on to say that Baldwin believed that meditation "improved his technical

search firm's productivity. Since his company started to meditate, revenues have increased and employees have clocked extra
billable hours. And employees say they notice the benefits on
the job: a greater ability to focus on tasks and less worry about
outcomes."

No other century has had to cope with the challenges we
face. Many of us lead intensely competitive lives, often focused
on material goals. Sport is big business, a competition of
endorsement contracts and bonus clauses rather than a game
played for enjoyment and recreation. The technology that links
us to others around the world also threatens to drown us with
information overload. Our ecological and social challenges are
frighteningly complex, and the potential for global cataclysm
looms. We know very well that we cannot continue along the
path we have been traveling.

Unless we pay attention to the imbalance between the
demands of the outside world and our largely untapped inner
potential for intuition and contentment, we are headed for
catastrophe. As Albert Einstein said, "The world we have created today has problems which cannot be solved by thinking
the way we thought when we created them."

Yet we also have an advantage no other century has enjoyed.
The wisdom of the ages is as close as any bookstore. For the
first time in history, we have access to the world's ancient spiritual traditions as well as more than a century of Western psychology. What we need is a way to put that wisdom to use so
that we can rediscover our inner talents and capabilities, our
essential inner intelligence.

Meditation can help us do this. "There is only one journey.
Going inside yourself," said the German poet Rainer Maria
Rilke. It is possible to live life meditatively, starting right now.

Meditation is a radical step in taking responsibility for our
own happiness. We need it more than ever. Meditation can

give us the security of an inner anchor, a touchstone of sanity in an increasingly crazy world. It can smooth the rough edges of our everyday lives, teach us how to love ourselves and others better, and help us attain the serenity and joy we seek.

What Is Meditation?

Meditation is not a thought, it is an experience.
—OSHO

I was driving along a sunny road in Sausalito one day many years ago, thinking about my upcoming lunchtime get-together with an old friend, when my reverie was interrupted by the wailing of a police siren behind me. After pulling me over, the police officer informed me that he had been following my car for some time and that I had been driving over the speed limit. I was shocked and desperately tried to justify myself, but he was already writing up the ticket—my second in three months. Something inside me suddenly woke up.

I had not noticed I was being tailed because I was too busy thinking about what I would talk about with my friend. If I continued like this I would soon lose my license. The ticket was like a ray of sunshine piercing my fog of unconsciousness. When I was sitting in meditation the following morning, I asked my inner wisdom why I had gotten the ticket. The reply came that I had to make driving a meditation. In other words, I had to be present behind the wheel, relaxed and alert, aware of what was happening around me on the road and streets, and aware of my body. This changed my whole attitude toward driving. I used to treat it as a chore; now I find that I really enjoy it. Driving is no longer an out-of-body experience; in fact it has become one of my daily meditations. I always leave in plenty of time and have learned to pay attention, to really be doing what I am doing: that is, driving my car. I am happy to say that I have not received a single ticket since that day.

I tell this story to illustrate that *meditation is not something apart from everyday life; it is a quality, a way of being.* The purpose of meditating is not to cut ourselves off from life, but rather to enter more deeply and fully into it. Certainly there are meditation techniques that we might do for an hour or ten or five minutes a day, but they are simply means to connect us with ourselves, to put us in touch with qualities we all have inside of us: relaxation, humor, compassion, awareness, self-acceptance, clarity of mind, and our inner silence. The time we set aside to practice our meditation method of choice is simply a reminder that we want to be more in touch with these qualities on an ongoing basis. And the more in touch we are, the more our lives become infused with a meditative quality. As the great Zen master and author of *Zen Mind, Beginner's Mind* Shunryu Suzuki said, "Meditation is not some kind of excitement but concentration on our usual everyday routine; when your practice is calm and ordinary, everyday life itself is enlightenment."

One way to access these qualities is through the disciplined practice of one of the many meditation methods that have been developed and passed down over the centuries. Like a scientist observing data, we can use these methods as a way of simply *observing* what's going on inside us, without judgment.

For centuries people have been on a quest of self-inquiry in search of inner peace and inner harmony. There have been many who have attained this "enlightenment": a presence of joy and creativity in everyday life, an ability to "see" into the reality of things and be awake to who they really are. How did they do it? They discovered a method that worked and continually practiced that method until it brought them what they wanted. For example, Jabbar, a Sufi mystic, created gibberish and many of his disciples became enlightened by chanting gibberish. Hotei, the Japanese mystic sometimes known as the Laughing Buddha, chose laughter and taught his disciples to laugh their way to enlightenment. Buddha created Vipassana, a technique of witnessing and watching the breath.

With your own continued practice you will get to understand yourself, to know your preferences. To quote Robert Louis Stevenson: "To know what you prefer instead of humbly saying Amen to what the world tells you you ought to prefer, is to keep your soul alive."

The mind likes to control. It tries to control the present and the future by relying on old ways of doing things. Meditation, by contrast, frees us from the mind. It frees us from the bondage of our conditioning—of old, set ways of thinking. By making us more alert, it gives us an ability to "watch" the mind and be aware of new possibilities, to find our own preferences, our own unique ways of doing things. By bringing our attention inward, it opens the doorways of the subconscious and allows the creativity that lies within us to emerge. Most things that we do in life we do through the mind. So when we turn inward, we think we have to use the mind, but meditation gives us a rare chance to disidentify with our minds. It helps us lay claim to our inner wisdom.

Wherever you are, whenever you think of it, say to yourself, "I am." Not your name, your work, your job title, or your nationality, but just "I am." This is what the Hindus call self-remembrance, what Buddha called right-mindfulness, what Gurdjieff called self-remembering, what Krishnamurti called awareness. If you forget to do it, don't judge yourself; just catch hold of the thread of it whenever you remember to do so.

Over time, the thread will become more constant; a continuity will arise. Through this remembrance, this mindfulness, you will start to find yourself, your authentic self.

Of course, we all have to find a place to begin. We don't become expert overnight; meditation is a process. My daily driving meditation, for instance, is always teaching me new things. I remember one cool fall day at a San Francisco parking garage. I stopped my car at the entrance, as directed, but failed to leave my keys in the ignition. The attendant could not, of course, move the car, so it sat there blocking the entryway until my return. When I finally returned to the garage, for a split second I wondered why my car was still sitting there. Then the truth dawned on me: In spite of a huge sign, and a reminder from the attendant, I had taken my keys with me. My mind had been elsewhere; I had not been paying attention. As I paid the fine, I noticed my anger rising for being so "out of it," so disconnected from the present moment. Allowing the anger to pass and remembering to be compassionate with myself helped me see the fine as a wake-up call, and I realized, with my returning sense of humor, that at least I was making some progress! A parking ticket is not only cheaper than a moving violation but reflects a more benign lapse of awareness than daydreaming while driving.

Meditation is a process of bringing awareness to ourselves at any given moment with humor, compassion, relaxation, and self-acceptance. It's a gift we can give ourselves to lighten up and bring a more expansive quality to our daily lives. Trying to explain what meditation is is like trying to explain what love is, but as you begin your own practice you will discover the multifaceted diamond that is meditation.

Part Two

MODERN MEDITATIONS TO FREE THE MIND AND UNLEASH THE SPIRIT— AT WORK, AT HOME, AT PLAY

1 ✦ It's Easier Than You Think: Relaxing

TO AFFECT THE QUALITY OF THE DAY, THAT IS THE HIGHEST OF ARTS.

—HENRY DAVID THOREAU

Meditation is based on relaxation: a feeling of physical, mental, and emotional ease, of resting inside ourselves. Relaxation begins with the body. We cannot relax if our bodies are full of the tensions and stresses of the day. All the meditation techniques I teach begin with the body, with bringing awareness to our bodies and moving into a state of relaxed awareness. As you will see, these techniques are nothing mysterious; they are activities that we already know how to do, such as jogging, dancing, humming, laughing. When we move into meditation by first releasing tension in the body, the process of coming to inner stillness goes much easier. Always begin with the body because that is where you are. It is important to begin where you are—not where you think you should be.

When we are small and learning to walk, we are totally present with each step, totally conscious that right now we are putting the right foot in front of the left foot. We are in our bodies. As we get the hang of it and the body acquires the knack of walking, we go on automatic. We are not present anymore with the walking; the body knows how to do it and we are somewhere else. We become disconnected from our bodily movements. As James Joyce wrote in *Dubliners* of his character Mr. Duffy, "he lived a short distance from his body."

To be beneficial, meditation must be grounded in the body.

There is a Hasidic tale of the great rabbi who was coming to visit a small town in Russia. It was a very great event for the Jews in the town and each thought long and hard about what questions they would ask the wise man. When he finally arrived, all were gathered in the largest available room, and each was deeply concerned with the questions they had for him. The rabbi entered the room and felt the great tension in it. For a time he said nothing and then began softly humming a Hasidic tune. Presently everyone hummed with him. He then began to sing a song and soon all sang with him. Then he began to dance and soon all present were caught up in the dance with him. After a time all were deeply involved in the dance, all fully committed to it, just dancing and nothing else. In this way, each one became whole with himself, healing the splits within which kept him from understanding. After a time, the rabbi slowed this dancing to a stop, looked at the group, and said, "I trust I have answered all your questions."

By complete absorption in bodily movement we are brought slowly and gradually to doing just one thing at a time. As we move out of our heads and into our bodies, all our questions can disappear and just enjoyment of the activity remains. An effective way to relax the mind and begin meditating is with a bodily activity. If the body does not feel the benefit, then your heart, mind, and soul will not either. The techniques are to help you come to an effortless moment: just being, doing nothing, relaxing into the present moment.

Relaxation cannot be forced, it is more a nondoing, an

allowing, a just being. It is a state of let go. To illustrate to you what I mean, imagine you are holding a tennis ball in your hand. Now try to drop it. Of course you cannot, because all you have to do is open your hand and let go. The same is true of relaxing into meditation. You just open yourself up, let go, and drop down inside yourself.

The techniques that follow will assist you in opening up and letting go of, for example, your frustrations, tensions, restlessness. When you try to relax, a subtle tension is created. So in this chapter we'll look at shifting the emphasis from "trying" to "letting go."

As you make a practice of relaxing you may gain some understanding of how you keep yourself busy or of how obsessive you are about staying in some activity. The more relaxed you are, the more you allow insights and understandings to arise. This awakening to who you are is the heart of meditation. It might take some practice, but once you start setting aside some time to do nothing, much will be revealed to you about yourself.

A FEW SIMPLE
RELAXATION TECHNIQUES

The following short techniques (none of these takes more than a few minutes to do) are some of the best I know for relaxing, grounding, and bringing body awareness. They require no special equipment or skill. I suggest you simply read through them all and try the one or ones that sound most appealing. Once you find the techniques that you particularly enjoy, you can begin to build them into your day or week. Don't be deceived by their simplicity; all of these techniques have a powerful ability to help reduce everyday anxiety and stress and bring an undercurrent of calm and peace to your

day. You might want to reread the information about sitting postures
on page 13. Another great relaxation technique called Nadabrahma
can be found on page 110. Also you might want to try my *Guided
Relaxation* tape. (See information for ordering on page 194.)

Breathe

One of the simplest and most effective practices for bringing us fully
into the present is conscious breathing—just remembering to come
back to the breath, to breathe in and out, in and out, in a steady way.
When we are tense or anxious our breathing becomes shallow;
sometimes we even stop breathing for short periods without realizing it. The simple act of conscious breathing brings us out of our
heads and into our bodies, into the present. It is one of the quickest
ways of dissolving tension and relaxing the mind and body.

Here we have this marvelous and powerful tool at our disposal at all
times, and yet it's so hard for most of us to get in the habit of using it.

Whenever you remember, wherever you are, just bring your
awareness to your breathing. Breathing in, breathing out. Yes, it's that
simple. Try it right now.

Relax the Breathing

This one is a slight variation on the "Breathe" technique. It is done
sitting.

Whenever you find time, just for a few minutes, sit down and
relax your breathing system. This is a great one to do whenever you
sit for long periods—in your car, on the bus or train, at your desk.
Just bring your awareness to your breathing. Nobody else will know
that you are doing anything. Simply let your breathing be as natural
as possible. Then, if possible, close your eyes and watch your breath
going in, coming out, going in.

Try not to concentrate. Concentrating creates a subtle tension in the body and then anything can disturb you. (People often think of meditation as concentration. It isn't concentration; it's awareness.) Simply relax and watch the breathing. In that watching nothing is excluded. People will be talking, telephones ringing, doors opening and closing, traffic passing; that's okay. It's all a part of life. Don't reject; just accept. This technique will bring you a respite of deep relaxation.

Stand on the Earth

Another wonderful way of coming into the present is by connecting with the earth. Whenever you can, just stand on the earth with bare feet and feel the softness, the coolness, the warmth of the earth under your feet. We spend so much time in our heads; it's easy to become ungrounded. Become aware of your feet and your connection to the earth. Whatever the earth is ready to give in that moment, feel it and let it flow through you. Allow your energy to flow into the earth. Feel the connection. Feel the life force.

It is best to do this without shoes, of course, but if it is not possible to go without shoes, then do it with shoes. Try to stand directly on earth, but if that is not possible, then just come as close to the ground as possible. If you are in an office or live in an apartment, then feel your feet on the floor. The important thing is to bring your attention to your feet and a feeling of grounding.

This technique can bring a deep sense of calm and peace. It's amazing what touching the earth can do to bring us back to center. It only takes a few moments to make this grounding connection but its benefits will carry throughout your day.

Look at the Sky

You know the phrase, "the sky's the limit"? Think for a moment about the feelings that are conjured up when you hear that phrase. Like the sky itself, it feels expansive, full of possibility, positivity, and enthusiasm, without limits, as if an unbounded goodness awaits you.

The next time the opportunity arises, lie down on the ground and look at the sky. Meditate on it. Enjoy its vastness, its beauty, its constancy. Realize how infinite it is, how compassionate.

Try "looking" at the sky with closed eyes. Feel your inner sky, your own expansiveness, vastness, beauty, and silence. If you want to pray, pray to the sky; if you want to meditate, meditate on the sky.

Do this technique for as long as you like—ten, fifteen, thirty minutes—and as often as you remember to do it. It will calm you; it will bring you in touch with your innermost self; it will help to remind you that life's rich bounty awaits you.

Sit Under a Tree

If you're trying to get grounded, there's no better way to do it than by sitting under a tree with your eyes closed. Try it. Feel the breeze as it passes through the tree, rustling the leaves and the branches. The wind touches you, moves around you, and passes you. Now allow it to move within you and pass through you. With your eyes closed as the wind is passing through the tree, feel that you are also like a tree, open, and the wind is blowing through you—not passing by your side but right through you.

Something as simple as this quick five- or ten-minute technique can be wonderfully effective at helping you to feel more rooted in yourself, more grounded, and at the same time more open, receptive, and relaxed.

Ten-Minute Sitting

Meditation decreases oxygen consumption, heart rate, respiratory rate, and blood pressure, and increases the intensity of alpha, theta and delta brain waves—the opposite of the physiological changes that occur during the stress response.

—HERBERT BENSON, M.D.
Harvard Medical School

This ten-minute sitting is a simple breathing method to stop the oversecretion of the adrenal glands, thus lowering blood pressure, reversing fatigue, and revitalizing the body's store of energy.

Sit in a comfortable position on a chair or on the floor. Make sure that your clothing is not constricted so your body can relax. Sit with the back relatively straight. Close your eyes. Bring your awareness to the inside of your body and begin to observe your breathing—the inhale and the pause at the top of the cycle; then the exhale and the pause at the bottom of the cycle. There is no right or wrong way to breathe so you don't have to change your breathing; just observe it.

Continue this for five, fifteen, or even thirty minutes. When you stop, notice if your body feels different. Generally after five or ten minutes you can actually feel the effects of the diminished adrenaline flow.

This method can be used throughout the day, anytime you need to revitalize.

WORKOUT MEDITATIONS

The following techniques build on our physical workout routines. Transforming your workout into a meditation simply takes a shift in awareness. Many people still hang on to the idea that meditation has to be done quietly and in stillness, that activity and meditation can't mix. I'd like to put those ideas to rest once and for all. *Any* activity can become a meditation if it is done with awareness.

Actually, movement *facilitates* awareness. Think about it: It's much easier to stay alert when you're moving than when you're sitting or lying down. The big challenge is to keep from going on automatic pilot, to keep from becoming mechanical. You may be a phenomenal runner, but if it's all technique, you've missed the point.

If you're a runner, try running with awareness; if you work out at a gym, trying working out with awareness; if you're a jogger, try jogging with awareness. Or if you feel that your workout has become too routine, try something different. Whenever we are learning something new, or are not yet expert at it, we have to pay more attention; we have to be more aware. Experiment with a movement that creates awareness in you. Dancing, perhaps. *The point to remember is that the movement is just a situation to create awareness.* Once it stops creating awareness then it is of no use to you anymore. Change to another activity where you will have to be alert again.

Running

Humans have been running for thousands of years, since we were hunters, and when we start running the body/mind engages with that primal layer of consciousness. Running can be an especially powerful tool for meditators; it creates a possibility to go very deep into ourselves.

If you are new to running, I would recommend that you run in the mornings, when the air is fresh and the day is just coming alive. Of course you want to consider any health problems you might have and speak with your doctor if you have any questions about whether or not you should run. It's also very important that you wear good running shoes.

Start with a half mile, then one mile, then build it up to at least three miles. Run using your whole body, including your hands. Breathe deeply and from the belly.

When you are running fast, breathing deeply, inhaling, exhaling, after a while the division between mind and body starts to disappear. You become one: one unity. When you are running and the breathing has taken hold of you, worries suddenly disappear. You just cannot be fully engaged with running and worried at the same time.

Jogging

Jogging follows the same principle as running. You want to breathe deeply and stay aware that "right now I am jogging." Again, I'd recommend jogging in the early morning. (Jogging can also be helpful at the end of the day to rid yourself of the day's tensions.) Enjoy the freshness of the day filling your lungs as you breathe deeply. If your mind starts wandering come back to the breathing and inhabit your body. As your body builds up a sweat, feel yourself becoming one with your body and the mind disappearing. This is the body's opportunity to take over, at least temporarily, from the mind.

Working Out at the Gym

If you prefer the gym, my recommendation would be to try to develop a routine. Without a routine, it's too easy to drift—five minutes on this machine, five minutes on that machine—without ever dropping down deep. Having a routine also makes it harder to come up with excuses (you're too busy, you'd rather be having coffee, you've got another appointment). The specifics of your routine don't matter so much as that you have one.

Working out is an opportunity to be with yourself. Close your eyes, become aware of your breathing, inhabit your body, come into present time. Perhaps short shallow breaths will be needed at the beginning, then deeper breaths. Be alert with yourself. Your breathing will bring you down from the head and into the body. If you become aware of any emotions, for example anger, sadness, let the body express them and release them. Give your mind a break and let the body take over.

Notice if you go on automatic, the body running on the treadmill and the mind back in the office. Gently remind yourself to come back into the body; focus on the breathing if this helps. Remember to practice nonjudgment and compassion for yourself. Slowly, slowly you can transform your exercising into meditation.

Use movement and exercise as a means to get in touch with deeper parts of yourself and you will enter more easily and fully into meditation.

MOVING MEDITATIONS

We've now come to some of my favorite techniques, the moving meditations. Like the running, jogging, and exercising techniques, these techniques should shatter any preconceptions you might have that meditation necessitates sitting in silence in the lotus posture.

All these meditations start with the body or its physical activity. Movement allows for the cathartic or physical release of tension from the body/mind and is a wonderful way to make the transition to sitting or lying down in stillness and silence.

The five meditations that follow were originally developed by my teacher Osho, exactly for the purpose of releasing tensions before dropping deeper down into meditation. They all involve movement, though not of the type you'd find at the gym. The Dancing and Shaking meditations are great for releasing physical stress and tension; the Gibberish and Dynamic meditations help release pent-up emotions and mental stress, including anger and frustration. Because insomnia has its roots in our inability to relax and turn off the mind, I've included here as well the Insomnia meditation, which builds on the Gibberish technique.

I suggest you try the moving meditations one at a time and give each one at least a week before you try another. Then settle into a routine with the practices that you like best.

Dancing

Have you ever put on your favorite dancing music when no one was around and just cut loose? If you haven't tried it, it's a great way to release tension or unwind. With a few simple additions, this pleasurable experience can become a meditation.

Historically, Sufis have a tradition of dancing as a meditation in celebration of life. The following dancing meditation created by Osho is called "Osho Nataraj." You can find information on ordering the *Osho Nataraj* CD that was created for this meditation on page 193. If you choose not to order the CD, I would suggest doing this one to any inspiring and celebratory music you like, but keep to the same selection. As Osho used to say, the important thing is to always do this meditation to the *same* music. That way it is easier to notice how your experience of the meditation changes each time.

You can do this meditation any time of day. It will take about sixty-five minutes. Try it especially if you are having trouble coming to stillness when you meditate. Dancing into meditation is a great way to direct your energy inward.

STAGE ONE: *Dancing (40 minutes)*

Clear a space where you can dance safely with your eyes closed. Put on the *Nataraj* CD or a CD of your own choosing. Close your eyes or cover them with a blindfold and dance for forty minutes. Let go of any sense of control and disappear into the dance. Allow your body to respond to the music any way it likes, from wild to very slow and gentle movements. Celebrate yourself. Become like a child again in love with movement for its own sake. No one can see you, and this experience is not about performing or looking good, which always creates a subtle tension. If feelings arise, express them through the dance. You have complete freedom to do any movement you and your body want.

Let the sense that you are *observing* yourself dance fall away naturally. You and the movement and the music are one. Dancing is no longer a *doing* but a *happening*.

As you continue to dance, you may start to forget that *you* are dancing and begin to feel that you *are* the dance. Unlike those times when you are still aware of the separation between yourself and the dance, between yourself and the music, it becomes a meditation when the divisions dissolve, when you are totally involved, totally merged into the dance. You do not need to do anything to force this shift; just follow the movement and the music and allow it to happen.

STAGE TWO: *Stillness (20 minutes)*

The next stage of the meditation is silent. Turn off the music and immediately lie down for twenty minutes. The *Osho Nataraj* CD includes this twenty minutes of silence, but if you don't have the CD, simply set a timer and, keeping your eyes closed, be totally silent and still.

STAGE THREE: *Get Up and Dance Again (5 minutes)*

To complete the meditation, turn on the music again and dance for five minutes. Celebrate and enjoy your body and the sense of total freedom dancing like this gives you.

Through the dancing meditation, a tremendous amount of tension is released, and creative insights may arise. Why this happens is no big mystery. Tension is simply trapped energy. The wild and free movement of the dance is a great way to set this energy free and get it moving. Feeling free in your body allows your mind to expand, your heart to open, and your spirit to fly. Then, when you lie still immediately after dancing, your gross level of activity—the body—is stopped, and the energy you have released travels inward to the more subtle layers of your being. This technique allows the dynamism of the dance to move to your roots, to the very core of your being, often liberating great feelings of joy and positivity. I recommend that you try this one any time you need the release.

Shaking

In this technique, we begin with the body, shaking it. "Shaking is so active, so deliberate—how can it be a meditation?" my students sometimes ask. Shaking is in fact a warm-up process. The idea is to loosen up and shake out all the tensions from the body/mind that have accumulated during the course of the day. It's important not to force the shaking or it will become just like a physical exercise—the body will be shaking but you will be like a rock within. Just allow it to happen, as if nobody is *doing* it.

As the shaking takes over it will begin to penetrate to the very core of your being. The vibrations will reach to your very center. Your whole body will become a turmoil of energy, a cyclone. This is continued in the second stage. Through the energy of the cyclone you can then reach to the center.

This is a preparation for the third and fourth stages, when you will be silent and still, open to receive the guest of meditation.

You know how musicians spend time before they play, tuning their instruments, checking their guitar strings or the sound of the drums, preparing before they actually play the music? Shaking is like that. It is a preparation, a "getting in tune" with ourselves so that when we sit the tensions will be dissolved and the space of meditation will descend upon us.

This shaking meditation, which Osho created and called "Osho Kundalini," is done in four stages of fifteen minutes each, so you'll want to set aside an hour for it. This is one of my favorite techniques for releasing mental, physical, and emotional stress at the end of the workday, especially after a long day of sitting staring at the computer screen. You can obtain the *Osho Kundalini* CD (see page 193 for ordering information) or simply set a timer to mark the different stages. I do not recommend substituting any other music.

STAGE ONE: *Shake It (15 minutes)*

Standing comfortably, eyes open or closed, just let your whole body shake, feeling the energies moving up from your feet. Let go and feel yourself become the shaking.

STAGE TWO: *Dance (15 minutes)*

Just let your body move any way it wishes. Dance.

STAGE THREE: *Becoming Still (15 minutes)*

Now, either sitting or standing, close your eyes and be still. Notice whatever's happening inside you and out. Relax deep within yourself. Be aware of your breathing, witness the thoughts of the mind, any emotions or feelings, with no judgment. Don't cling or reject, simply accept what is. Allow the silence of meditation to descend upon you.

STAGE FOUR: *Lie Down and Be Still (15 minutes)*

Now, without opening your eyes, lie down. Just lie there in stillness for another fifteen minutes.

When I do this meditation I find it helpful, in the first stage, to imagine myself as a rag doll shaking out all the tensions from the body/mind, remembering in particular to shake my head a lot if I have had a very mentally stressful day. I like to keep my feet firmly planted on the ground so that I stay rooted in myself and don't tip over. I find that this allows me to experience greater flexibility of movement in the shaking. It's a good idea to keep your knees slightly bent, remembering to shake the legs, hips, upper torso, shoulders, arms, hands, and head. This is an extraordinarily gentle yet powerful way to release stress and free up the body from any straightjacket it has been in—sitting driving the car or in front of the computer.

The sense of freedom carries over into the second stage. You can use the dance to release and express any emotional stress such as frustration, anger, sadness, disappointment and also express any playfulness, happiness, and joy you might be in touch with that particular day. It is surprisingly refreshing to be able to get in touch with ourselves nonverbally and allow the more hidden or repressed parts some space to be there, to come out into the open. This is a great way to get to know ourselves and gain clarity and insight into whatever is going on in our lives at the present time.

After all the physical expression and release, to then sit or stand is both relaxing and an opportunity to witness whatever is happening with ourselves, compassionately and without judgment.

Finally, when we lie down in silence, the body, fully supported by the floor, can sink into a deep relaxation. This depth of relaxation allows the energy generated by the first two stages to take our meditation to the deepest corners of our being.

If you like this technique, try to do it every day, or as often as you can find the time. The best time to do it is at the end of the day, when you get home from work. It's a great way to literally shake off the tensions of the day, leaving you refreshed to enjoy your evening. It can also bring you insight and clarity about your workday.

Gibberish

Gibberish was first used hundreds of years ago by a Sufi mystic named Jabbar. In fact the very word "gibberish" derives from his name. It is said that people would come to Jabbar with all kinds of questions about enlightenment and he would simply answer with nonsense sounds. At first people thought he was crazy and that no one would come to listen. But hundreds of people came and he ended up having more disciples than any other mystic of his time.

What was happening was really something great. Listening to Jabbar your mind had nothing to do. You couldn't agree or disagree with him because he was just talking nonsense, a constant stream of sounds and words with no commas or periods, no sentence structure.

Jabbar enjoyed himself very much and would laugh as if he were telling jokes and then he would start up again. By and by the disciples, who continually increased in number, realized that just by sitting near Jabbar, listening to his gibberish, their minds became more and more silent. And that was his whole purpose: to bring them into a state of meditation, to bring them into touch with their own inner silence. This great mystic answered their questions by taking them deep inside themselves, beyond the mind where their own answers lay.

The mind thinks in terms of words. Gibberish helps to break up this pattern of continuous verbalization. Without suppressing your thoughts, you can throw them out using the Gibberish meditation. It is a wonderful way to release physical, mental, and emotional stress.

The technique you'll learn here is based on a version I learned from my teacher Osho. You can do it at any time of day. To start with you might want to try five minutes of gibberish followed by five minutes of silence. Then build up to fifteen, twenty, thirty, or even an hour of gibberish followed by the equivalent time of silent sitting. If you like you can use my *Gibberish Meditation* tape to accompany you. (See page 194 for more information.) I would suggest that you eat lightly beforehand. You will be moving a lot of tensions out of the body/mind and having a full stomach might make you nauseated.

Find someplace to do it where you won't feel at all self-conscious. I recommend that you wear a blindfold. Sometimes, with the more cathartic techniques, the eyes can fly open involuntarily and the blindfold can keep you from getting distracted by anything going on around you.

STAGE ONE: *Gibberish*

Close your eyes and just start speaking in gibberish, nonsense sounds. Don't worry about what you sound like, just go totally mad.

Make any sounds you like; just don't speak in a language or use words that you know. Allow yourself to express whatever needs to be expressed within you. Go consciously crazy.

Do it any way you like: sing, cry, shout, scream, mumble, talk. Let your body go free, too. Allow it to express itself any way it wants, especially if you've been cooped up in an office all day. You may want to stamp, stomp, jump, skip, lie down, run in circles. Do whatever you feel like doing without harming anyone. Do not let up. You should be moving and talking in a steady stream. You don't want any empty spaces. If no other sounds come, say, "blah blah blah," but you don't want any silences during this one.

If you are doing this meditation with other people, try not to be distracted by what they're doing or to interfere with them in any way. Just stay with what is happening with you.

STAGE TWO: *Witnessing*

Set a timer for the time period you've chosen. When the ringer goes off, *stop* and *freeze* for a moment. Listen to the silence after all the noise and babbling. Then find a place to sit comfortably, either the floor or a chair; it doesn't matter. Close your eyes and breathe naturally. Your head and back should be straight but not rigid. Just sit there in stillness and silence, gathering your energy inward. Let thoughts just drift away and feel yourself falling into the deep silence and peacefulness that is at your center.

Try to be totally in the present moment, just witnessing whatever passes by without judgment. If you feel your thoughts racing ahead to your next activity or back to the past, just try to watch them from a distance—don't judge them; don't get caught up in them. Just stay in the present, watching. What you are watching is not important, it's the process of watching that is the meditation.

The gibberish technique isn't just for releasing stressful emotions such as anger, frustration, or rage. You can also use it to express and enjoy positive emotions such as joy or excitement. You might find yourself playful and clowning around having a lot of fun, experimenting with different parts of yourself. You can try anything from growling like a jungle animal to speaking an imaginary foreign language. Be outrageous. This is not about making sense; it's about learning to lighten up. Even a few minutes of acting ridiculous can bring a surprising amount of relief.

I often suggest to people that they try postures and sounds that are new to them. This is helpful in accessing creativity and releasing us from "in the box" thinking. This is one way we can break free from old conditionings and discover unlimited possibilities within ourselves. Enjoy.

Dynamic Meditation

The Dynamic meditation was designed for those of us who enjoy a good physical workout. It is perfect for our hyped-up lives, having little to do with the stereotypical idea of bald-shaved monks sitting for hours on cold stone floors contemplating holy matters. Its message is simple: release your mental, emotional, and physical stress so that you can become physically engaged with enjoying your life *now*. It is the most vigorous technique in this section and extremely powerful in cutting through any blocks in the body/mind to bring you to your essential self.

This technique was created by Osho. A special soundtrack *Osho Dynamic* was created for it (see page 193 for ordering information), and I particularly recommend this one because the drumming and music urge you on past the temptation to quit. If you can't get hold of the CD, you can do just fine by setting a timer for the different stages. I do not recommend substituting any other music.

The words "dynamic" and "meditation" used together present us with an interesting contradiction. The word "dynamic" suggests effort, tremendous effort, and the word "meditation" implies silence, no effort. Yet it is in this very contradiction that we have a possibility to bring ourselves into balance.

This meditation has five stages. The first three—breathing, catharsis, and the Sufi mantra "Hoo!"—are designed to get us in touch with our vital energy source, our aliveness, our vibrancy. They allow for complete release and expression and should be done with vigor, so that no energy is left static in you. The idea is to exhaust your outgoing energy. When the mind has no more energy for creating thoughts, dreams, and imaginings, when it is absolutely spent, you will find that you are *in*.

The fourth stage involves silent witnessing. Coming on the heels of the first three stages, this silence is vital, alive, bubbling with life energy. It is a live silence that cannot be achieved by ordinary, rational effort. In the Zen tradition this is called "effortless effort." The use of a contradictory term suggests that the process is dialectical, not linear. The energy of the earlier stages is not denied but absorbed; it is *used*.

The fifth stage is celebration and dance.

This meditation is best done on an empty stomach in the early morning. Again, I would recommend wearing a blindfold to help you stay in your body without distraction. I try to blow my nose before starting this meditation to free up the passage of air through the nostrils. You'll need about sixty minutes for this one.

STAGE ONE: *Breathing (10 minutes)*

If you have the CD, put it on and, standing with neck and shoulders relaxed, begin breathing rapidly through the nose, letting your breath be intense and chaotic. (If you don't have the CD, I recommend that you do this without music.) Breathe as fast as you can while keeping the breaths deep. This is not shallow breathing. You should feel the breath deep in the lungs. Do this as totally as you possibly can. Keep your neck and shoulders relaxed.

Keep up this chaotic breathing. (It musn't take on a rhythm

because then you might go on automatic pilot. Keeping it chaotic helps to keep you in the present moment.) You can use your arms like a kind of bellows to help pump more energy through your chest and lungs until you literally *become* the breathing. Once your energy is moving, your body will begin to move as well. Let it happen. Use the movement to help you build up even more energy. Let your arms and body move naturally. This will help build the energy. Until the ten minutes are up, don't let up and don't slow down.

STAGE TWO: *Catharsis (10 minutes)*

Let it all out. Just totally cut loose. Jump, laugh, scream, cry, shake, kick, punch, whatever your body feels like doing. Don't hold back, just keep your whole body moving and the sounds coming. Let it all hang out. Don't let your mind interfere; just stay totally in your body. Go mad.

STAGE THREE: *Hoo! (10 minutes)*

With shoulders and neck relaxed, raise both arms as high as you can without locking the elbows. With raised arms, jump up and down, shouting the mantra Hoo! . . . Hoo! . . . Hoo! as deeply as possible, coming from the depths of your belly. Each time you land on the flats of your feet (without locking your knees and making sure heels touch the ground), let the sound hammer deep into your center. Give it all you've got. Exhaust yourself completely.

STAGE FOUR: *Silent Witnessing (15 minutes)*

Freeze! Stop wherever you are and in whatever position you find yourself. Don't arrange the body in any way. A cough, a movement, anything will dissipate the energy flow and the effort will be lost. Be a witness to everything that is happening to you.

STAGE FIVE: *Dance (15 minutes)*

Spend fifteen minutes celebrating your aliveness. Dance, expressing whatever is there. Bring this energy with you into your day.

With this technique, you want to open yourself as wide as possible for the breath of life; take in as much of it as you can possibly take. You want to stop philosophizing, stop dreaming of the day when you'll really start living. Do it now! *Live!*

Whenever I do the Osho Dynamic meditation, an exhilaration fills me. The deep fast breathing dissolves the cemented patterns in my psyche, making everything move and tingle, and charges my body with oxygen and life energy. Ah yes—this is great!

When I notice my halfheartedness I change to a higher gear. Within minutes I have reached a speed that leaves my thoughts panting behind. That is one of the purposes of the exercise: The mind is blown away—fear not, it will come back! All I hear now is a staccato of massive outbreaths. I realize that even more is possible (more is always possible) and breathe even more deeply. I think nothing; there is only breathing—deeper, faster, madder. It's totally far out. From a certain speed limit, a certain intensity on, I am simply in it, and it is fun to go for the maximum.

When the catharsis section starts, what a relief to express all my pent-up emotions, unburden my mind, and allow my body to release the built-up tensions. Urging myself on, I discover deeply buried layers of myself, opened up by the first stage, that need expression. Long forgotten anger, hurts, disappointments can surface and be thrown out. All kinds of old emotional "baggage" can be purged and released from my body and mind. By the third stage, I feel cleaned out and ready to fully shout the mantra "Hoo!" the sound arising loud and strong from deep within my belly. As the sound resonates through my whole body, I feel it continuing the work of the first two stages, shedding even more layers of tensions. My body/mind starts to feel like a hollow bamboo, preparing through this exercise to receive the silence of the fourth stage.

Suddenly I hear a voice shout "Stop" (if you don't have the CD, set a timer to ring to start the fourth stage); I freeze and listen to the silence. Fourth stage. I sink into a profound depth of stillness.

After all the noise and effort I stand stock still, just breathing, being, enjoying, witnessing. This is it! The moment I have been waiting for. Such joy to discover this vibrant silence pervading my whole body and to simply watch.

For the celebration dance of the fifth stage, I have plenty to celebrate. For one thing, one more Dynamic meditation accomplished. I celebrate myself, that I have been willing to put such effort into my journey of self-discovery, releasing my tensions and getting in touch with my creativity and enjoyment of life. I feel full of infinite possibilities, like an open sky.

Osho Dynamic meditation is a method for anyone who feels stressed out, neurotic, confused. It is an inner and outer workout that hews a new path through the jungle of our overly speedy minds. Many people like to learn to teach it and then introduce it as an early morning class in their local gym or at their work. As you well know, the more effort you put into something, the greater the payoff. Try this technique for at least twenty-one days. You will be richly rewarded.

Insomnia Meditation

Seventy-five percent of long-term insomniacs who have been trained in relaxation and meditation can fall asleep within twenty minutes of going to bed.

—DR. GREG JACOBS
Harvard psychologist

If you suffer from insomnia, I know of no better cure than meditation. Insomnia is usually caused by an overactive mind. The mind accumulates noise throughout the day and when you want to go to sleep it continues; it's become a habit. It does not know how to turn off. It's as if the switch isn't working. Getting to sleep, then, is a matter of finding a way to release this energy and then, emptied out, you will easily fall asleep. Through the following meditation, you create a situation in which that can happen easily.

Sit in your bed, turn the lights off, and start talking in gibberish. Do this for thirty minutes. Allow any sounds that come. Don't worry about meaning, language, grammar. In fact, the more meaningless your sounds, the more helpful they are. You are simply throwing out the rubbish that the mind collects during the day.

Just start and go. But be very passionate about it, as if your whole life depended on it. Be in a passionate dialogue with yourself. Put your whole energy into it. Do this for thirty minutes and chances are you will have a good night's sleep, if not the first night then in the nights to come.

The gibberish works so well because there's no judgment involved. You can't start analyzing or feeling guilty about what you're saying, or moralizing that you're saying bad things. When you speak in sounds you don't know what you are saying. Your gestures, your passion are doing the work.

Try this for at least seven days. The mind will become accustomed to the release, the unburdening of all this mental stress, and will welcome it. Afterward you will enjoy a good, natural sleep.

Remember, insomnia is a *symptom* of a greater stress in your life. If you have been in the habit of taking sleeping pills, you are only treating the symptom and not the underlying stress. Here are some other suggestions for dealing with insomnia:

+ Take a look at the stress factors in your daily life and remember that these could be mental, emotional, or physical, or a combination of the three. Read through all the relaxation techniques in this chapter. By incorporating relaxation techniques into your day, the underlying cause of your stress, and therefore your insomnia, can well be eliminated.

✦ Examine any possible physical reasons for your insomnia. For example, if you drink ten cups of coffee a day, or eat a heavy meal late at night, these can keep you awake. If you smoke, remember that nicotine is a powerful stimulant. Don't forget the high dose of caffeine in ordinary chocolate.

✦ Think about how you spend your evening. Watching TV can stimulate the nervous system. Try listening to relaxing music instead. Or try my *Insomnia Meditation* CD, a guided journey into sleep with soothing music (see page 194 for ordering information).

✦ After your workday, try some of the more energetic meditations. For example, jogging, running, shaking, or dancing meditations can be very helpful in releasing stress after a work day and bringing you to a more relaxed state.

Simple Reminders

Finally, here are some simple reminders to help you reinhabit your body and come into a state of relaxation. Try these anywhere, anytime you think of it. You might also like to try my CD *Wisdom of the Body Meditation* (see page 194 for ordering information).

1 ✦ Slow down every process.

   Try walking in a relaxed way, eating in a relaxed way, talking and listening in a relaxed way. Even if you are in a rush, try to rush in a relaxed way, with the awareness that "right now I am rushing."

2 ✦ Schedule regular time for relaxation.

Use "downtime," however short, for a relaxation break. For example, every time you stop at a red light, each time you're put on hold or find yourself waiting for someone, breathe slowly and deeply or think about what you're going to do for yourself next.

3 ✦ Use aromatherapy to help you relax.

The scent of essential oils extracted from plants can have a restorative effect on the body and mind. Lavender and chamomile oils are particularly good for relaxation.

4 ✦ Create a stress-free place for yourself at home.

Don't allow work or clutter . . . Make some place you can spend time when you need to relax. It doesn't even have to be inside—a porch or patio can be a great place to unwind.

5 ✦ Bring your awareness to your body.

Find a relaxing place to sit or lie down. Close your eyes. I would recommend listening to the music CD *Healing Touch* by Nadama (information on ordering the CD can be found on page 194) or some other music that is particularly relaxing to you. *Healing Touch* was specifically written to enhance healing and induce relaxation. Allow the music to wash over you and take you deeper and deeper into serenity and peace. Let the music comfort and soothe you. Just hang out in this relaxed state for fifteen minutes, or longer if you have time.

6 ✦ Release the tensions you are carrying.

As often as possible, remember to connect with your body and see if you are carrying tension somewhere. Then see if you can relax that part. You might like to try my CD *Transforming Tensions Meditation* (for information on ordering the CD see page 194). Or try one of the active meditations in this book; running, jogging, going to the gym, and movement meditations are all ways for the energy to be released.

Other ways of bringing awareness to the body include drinking water, taking walks, exercising, getting a massage, biking or hiking, and enjoying the fresh air and benefits of nature.

7 ✦ Try sauntering.

When outdoors, meander through woods, hillsides, or paths with no purpose, no goal, letting your instincts take you where they will. The celebrated writer Henry David Thoreau liked to wander aimlessly in the wilderness. "The walking of which I speak has nothing in it akin to exercise," he offered, "[I] submit myself to my instinct to decide for me." He called this sauntering, from the French *sans terre*, which means "without land or home."

8 ✦ Find the middle way.

Be careful with being too active or too inactive. If you become too active anxiety is created, a kind of rush, hurry, speed, restlessness. If you become too inactive you feel a kind of lethargy, indolence. Be in the middle.

9 ✦ Don't eat too much; don't eat too little.

Some people teach fasting, but fasting does not help meditation. In fact it hinders it. When you are hungry, how can you be in a still place? Eat so that you don't feel hungry, but don't eat too much so that you feel overloaded and sleepy. Meditation then will be easier.

10 ✦ Don't sleep too much; don't sleep less than needed.

It's important to get enough sleep so the body can regenerate itself. The mind also needs rest. Too much sleep can leave us feeling dull and heavy. By paying attention to the wisdom of your body, you will come to know the right amount of sleep for *you*. We each have to find our own unique balance. You might like to try my *Wisdom of the Body Meditation* CD (see page 194 for ordering information).

11 ✦ Drop all extremes.

Because only in the middle is a relaxed state of mind. If you can attain this kind of balance between effort and effortlessness, between purpose and purposelessness, between being and no being, between mind and no mind, between action and no action, then you learn to flow with the flow of things. You can let yourself go.

12 ✦ Try lounging.

Spend some time at home, not doing anything in particular. Move from one thing to the next, randomly, wherever your intuition wants to go. Clear out a drawer of socks, sit on the porch, dig around in the garden, call a friend, lie on the couch daydreaming, whatever takes your fancy, do it.

13 ✦ Try smiling gently when you breathe.

Smiling relaxes the muscles in the body. Try it right now.

14 ✦ Sit and do nothing for five minutes.

See if you can sit with no agenda, simply being. Over time, your busyness, your obsession with activity will simply fall away with the awareness of seeing how absurd it is. You will become at ease with yourself. You will find your way home.

15 ✦ Leave effort behind.

In the Zen tradition, the masters say to the disciples, "Just sit. Don't do anything." And the disciples try, because in the beginning, effort will be there. But by and by, when you remember constantly that you have to go beyond trying, a moment will come when you are not doing anything about meditation; just being there, aware, and it happens. The inner transformation cannot happen through effort because effort creates tension. But by making effort at the beginning, with the background of awareness, you will also become capable of leaving effort behind. This will happen of its own accord—it is not something you can control.

16 ✦ Be in the present moment.

Finally, remember, the more you can drop expectations, not desire anything to happen at all, accept the state of affairs as is, and just be, the more relaxed you will become. And the more relaxed you become, the deeper you can go in your inner journey.

2 ✦ The Laughing Buddha:
Enjoying Your Way to
Enlightenment

THE OLD MAN LAUGHED LOUD AND JOYOUSLY, SHOOK UP THE
DETAILS OF HIS ANATOMY FROM HEAD TO FOOT AND ENDED BY
SAYING SUCH A LAUGH WAS MONEY IN A MAN'S POCKET, BECAUSE
IT CUT DOWN THE DOCTOR'S BILLS LIKE EVERYTHING.

—MARK TWAIN

The Adventures of Tom Sawyer

I was sitting in a restaurant one Sunday evening enjoying my pasta salad and the company of some of my friends when the sounds of giggles and laughter drifted over from the table next to us. We turned to see a family with two teenage daughters who had a bad case of the giggles. The father was obviously not in a good mood and was becoming more and more exasperated with the girls who just couldn't contain their laughter. He finally said with a very serious straight face, "That's enough laughing for the weekend, Julia."

I had to turn away so he wouldn't see my grin. Julia, meanwhile, was trying to talk herself into starting on Monday's quota of laughter. Her rationale being that she would be at school and wouldn't be able to laugh as much as on a Sunday.

The absurdity of being given a ration of laughter each day reminded me of the way I was raised. Until then, I hadn't really thought much about how serious my upbringing had been. My laughter had been largely repressed. Giggling, laughing, and too much enjoyment were definitely frowned upon at school and church and other childhood places. I wasn't aware of just how much this had been repressed until I started doing the Mystic Rose meditation (see page 149). During the Mystic Rose, one spends a good deal of time just laughing. When I first tried it, it felt strange to laugh for three hours, especially in the presence of other people (the Mystic Rose is best done in a group). However, it didn't take long to get in the swing of it and then I found that my natural laughter just kept bubbling up to the surface.

Meditation isn't something you have to work at with a straight face. Be sincere about meditation, yes! but not serious, because then you will try to force and achieve. This will only create more tension. The more fun you have with the various techniques—the more playful you are as you approach them— the more relaxed you will be and the more you will want to keep meditating.

As Dr. Raymond Moody explains in *Laugh after Laugh: The Healing Powers of Humor:*

> Laughter is a good natural tranquilizer. It can stimulate the brain to produce hormones called catecholamines which may then trigger the release of endorphins. Endorphins have been described as a natural valium and foster a sense of relaxation and well-being. Catecholamines also enhance blood flow and thus may speed healing, reduce inflammation and stimulate alertness.

I present the approach of laughter, humor, and enjoyment of life here because no skill is needed, there is nothing to learn, there are no rules, it's something you already know how to do—it's simply a matter of degree, of bringing more lightness of spirit into your life.

We don't have to wait to be happy. The practices I've included in this chapter are a way to help us relax, loosen up, and enjoy life. They provide the opportunity for a playfulness, a reminder that life does not have to be a constant struggle. Even when we are not feeling happy, these techniques can help to energize us and move us forward in difficult times. They help coax to the surface our inner happiness, serving as a vehicle to awaken us to our innate joy.

Happiness is our essential nature. Rather than waiting for events outside of ourselves to determine our happiness, we can find the happiness which is our essential nature deep inside. We maybe think we have to be relaxed and calm and all sorts of conditions need to be there for us to be happy. This is not the case. Happiness can be there for no reason. The more we make a practice of smiling, laughing, enjoying ourselves *for no reason* the more we will discover that what we seek we already have.

Although many of us know that laughter is good for us, we might feel that we have nothing to laugh about, we may even feel more like crying. Whether we're going through a difficult phase in life, or just feel life is hard, laughing might seem too much of a struggle, too overwhelmingly difficult.

If this is the case, there is a much deeper practice at the end of the book called the Mystic Rose meditation (see page 149) that can be enormously helpful. It helps us heal in the present and let go of feelings and beliefs that may be blocking us from experiencing more love, gracefulness, flexibility, and enjoyment in our lives.

So try some of these laughter techniques but be kind and

gentle with yourself. If you don't feel like laughing, practice smiling more often, read some joke books, watch comedy movies or videos; then what is naturally inside will begin to surface more and more easily. And remember that if you are in a difficult time in your life, then also give an equal amount of time to allow your sadness to be there. *It is the balanced awareness and expression of both of these energies that will bring you to a deeper harmony and peace within yourself.*

The Benefits

Laughter is good for us in every way: physically, emotionally, spiritually. Among its many benefits:

Laughter stimulates physical healing. ✦ If you can laugh when you are ill you will get your health back sooner. If you cannot laugh, sooner or later you will become ill. Laughter brings energy from your inner source to your surface.

Laughter enhances our creativity. ✦ What I have noticed after numerous episodes of laughter is that as our energetic systems open up we are flooded with more creative energy. As old conditionings are released the unconscious opens and insights come. The relaxation of body and mind provides a gateway for the inner wisdom to come forward into expression.

Laughter is rejuvenating and regenerating and keeps us young. ✦ When we laugh and smile we loosen up and generally feel better. The face collects stress and when we laugh we can release a tremendous amount of tension from the face. This gives us a more youthful appearance. It reminds us about having fun. Maybe today, do something just for the sheer fun of it.

Laughter is sexy. ✦ It is an attractive energy vibration and can help bring people to you who are good for you. It is very beneficial for anyone who is sexually blocked. It releases inhibitions and opens up the energetic channels, bringing us directly in touch with our energy. Many people have told me of improved sexual responsiveness after doing the Laughter meditations.

Laughter is good for relationships. ✦ Humor draws people together. Many couples who do the Laughter meditation (page 63) and the Mystic Rose meditation (page 149) together tell me they find a tremendous improvement in their relating. They discover another side of each other, the playful, humorous side, which gives a relief to the more *serious* part of life concerned with work, money, housework, the kids, etc. Remember the old adage: "All work and no play makes Jack a dull boy"? Well, it doesn't do much for Jill either!

Laughter opens the heart. ✦ It creates an opening to the love, compassion, courage, trust, and intuitive wisdom that vibrates within you.

Laughter gives us a glimpse of freedom from the mind. ✦ For those moments when you are totally laughing, you are free of the mind. You are brought from worry to humor, from tension to relaxation, from fear to trust, from timidity to courage. In other words from the mind to the heart. You cannot think and laugh at the same time. In those seconds when you are out of the mind you are in meditation. In those seconds the mind is not and you are.

Hotei, the Laughing Buddha

The enlightened mystic most associated with laughter is Hotei; he is often known as the Laughing Buddha. Hotei was a large man with a big belly who traveled from village to village in sixteenth-century Japan. He had no desire to call himself a Zen master or to gather disciples. Instead, he walked the streets carrying a sack full of candy, fruit, and doughnuts, which he gave to all the children who gathered around him.

At first people would gather around him because they thought he was mad to laugh so much. But Hotei's laughter was so contagious that soon they all found themselves doubled over with laughter and they forgot all their judgments. Even when they would ask spiritual questions about enlightenment, Hotei would just laugh. Soon they forgot their questions, the laughter was so infectious.

It is said that Hotei even laughed in his sleep, that his whole body would shake as the laughter rumbled up from his belly. Hotei was very stout and strong because he laughed so much. Laughter was so natural to him that anything and everything helped him to laugh. This was his way of teaching enlightenment. And people could experience, as they shared the laughter with him, that they were in the presence of a master, that something of tremendous significance was transpiring. So he came to be known as the Laughing Buddha. He was a different type of master than the Buddha, but a Buddha nonetheless. He offered another way, through laughter. He was his own message, his very life was his teaching.

Hotei didn't laugh at jokes or at others. He laughed at himself. He laughed in celebration of existence, out of joy of life. And he was tremendously compassionate. He wanted to share his gift with as many people as possible. He wanted to see people's faces light up with laughter, see their beings become radiantly happy at the sheer joy of being alive.

He had no philosophy, no scriptures, no dogmas, theories, ideologies, concepts to preach. His teaching was existential. He wanted everyone to experience the joy laughter brings. It is not something that can be talked about. It must be experienced. This is meditation. Hotei was doing a tremendous service to humanity. He was not a philosopher. He was a very simple being, silent, happy, alive, living moment to moment.

The beauty of using laughter as a meditation is that it's not something that we have to go out in search of. Each of us is born full of laughter; it's just that in most of us it has been repressed. So all we have to do is allow it to arise again and cascade out of us.

So how do we intentionally bring ourselves to laughter? You might want to try my *Laughter Meditation* CD (see page 194 for ordering). Jokes are also a great place to start. They are never logical. If they were, we would be able to predict their outcome and the humor would be lost. Instead, they trigger a process in us that brings us totally into the present moment. We forget our seriousness, our problems, and for a moment we are innocent children again, full of wonder and awe.

The reason we laugh at jokes, the reason we find them funny is that they take sudden jumps and turns, so sudden that it is almost impossible for us to imagine it, and that's why they engender so much laughter. For example: My name is Jan Msikzmenthalyi. That's spelled J-A-N.

Suddenly we are all on the same wavelength; no one is the boss or the employee, the parent or the child, the lawyer or the banker; we are all one, joined in the common denominator of laughter. The laughter overwhelms us and drowns the ego. And whenever the ego disappears, we are at one with ourselves. The more we laugh, the deeper we can go into meditation. The energy of laughter acts as a channel to take us deep inside ourselves where our inner silence lies. It is such a strong force of energy that it can clear a path through the debris of unconscious conditioning and reunite us with ourselves.

LAUGHTER AND ENJOYMENT MEDITATIONS

Enjoy Yourself!

This technique is very simple: Only do that which you enjoy. Try this whenever you have an opportunity, maybe on your lunch break, or at the weekend at first. Enjoyment comes from the center, so whenever we are doing something we enjoy, we are centered, we feel a deep inner peace arising, a relaxation. So experiment. If you are walking along the road, bring your awareness to your activity: Are you enjoying your walk, or not? If not, then stop. Do something else.

Enjoyment is the sound of being centered. Whenever you are not enjoying something, you are off-center. So don't force anything, there is no need. Check in with yourself to determine whether you are doing something because it is a duty, or because you were taught to enjoy it or because you are really truly enjoying yourself. And the possibilities are vast and individual, so there is bound to be something that you will enjoy. The secret of this meditation is: that there be something you have started to enjoy. Because whenever you enjoy something you are in tune with yourself and you are in harmony with the universe. You are connected to your center, your inner haven of serenity. Then you will discover that what you are seeking is already within you, it has nothing to do with the future, it is already here now, it is already the case.

Smile Before Making a Call

Before you pick up the phone to make a call, smile. This is the energy you will send out. As you transmit friendliness and good will this simple practice will enhance all your business and personal communication. Try it. You might like to extend it to making a smiling practice for the day. Smile whenever you think of it. Perhaps try walking down the street with a smile on your face, not even smiling at anyone in particular. Notice how it makes you feel. Notice the effect upon others. This simple technique will transform the quality of your day.

The Laughter Meditation

In the morning when you wake up, stretch your body—every muscle, cell, and fiber in your body, just like a cat. After a few moments start laughing. Just start. At the beginning you may have to force it a little, saying "Ha, ha, ha," or "Ho, ho, ho" to get the energy of the laughter moving. Soon a spontaneous laughter will arise at the sound of your attempts at laughing. Try it for five minutes. Just laugh for no reason at all. Laugh for the sake of laughing. You might want to use my laughter CD (ordering information can be found on page 194) to help you get started.

Try it again for five minutes when you go to bed, just before you go to sleep.

At the beginning it will take some effort, but after a little while it will start to happen naturally. Your body will get used to it and start to expect it.

Try it in the shower, or while driving your car, stuck in traffic. Ha, ha, ha. Even to say those words out loud will start a transformation in your energy, in your mood. You might want to use my laughter tape.

Laughter is one of the easiest ways to find a nonthinking state, to find your inner being. It will make you more alive, more healthy, more creative, and more silent. Start laughing, especially first thing in the morning when you get up, and last thing at night when you go to bed. It will transform the quality of your day. It will transform the quality of your sleep. Laugh for no reason, at the whole ridiculousness of your life, of your day, rushing from here to there. It will create a chain effect; laughter leads to more laughter. Start and finish your day with laughter and watch as you become more easygoing, more sincere (but less serious), more creative, more youthful, more compassionate, more intuitive, more authentic, more expansive.

Simply relax into the enjoyment of it and let the flower of awareness bloom in its own time and in its own way. You will discover in yourself a tremendous natural talent for rejoicing in life. You may even laugh your way to enlightenment. Yes, it's that good. Remember to laugh—a lot—every day.

Joke Book at Bedtime

This is a variation of the laughter meditation. I find it particularly effective in times of great stress.

Keep a joke book by your bedside. Before turning out the lights at bedtime, sit silently for a few minutes breathing with awareness, watching any thoughts and emotions, and noticing how your body is feeling. Smiling gently as you breathe is very relaxing for the body.

Read the jokes for ten minutes (or longer), keeping a smile on your face even if you are not laughing at all the jokes and maintaining a mood of amusement and fun. If you are feeling particularly stressed and nothing is feeling very funny, start with stretching your lips into a smile. Simply doing this will have a powerful effect on starting to relax you on the inside. Gradually you will feel your inner smile surfacing to match your outer smile. Focus on the jokes, not thinking about anything else, only the jokes. Soon you will find yourself laughing and all your worries will disappear.

You will fall asleep bathed in laughter and humor. This will stay with you all night long, working on deeper layers of your consciousness. After a while, as you make a practice of this, you will find yourself waking up in the morning after a sound night's sleep in a wonderful humor, full of positivity, looking forward to your day. You will also find your sense of humor during the day is more readily available.

Start a Laughter Club

In India, many people gather together before work, in the mornings, and laugh. They stand in the busy, crowded street in their business suits and laugh. They have many of these laughter clubs throughout the country. Why don't you start one? You could get together before work, or perhaps as a Lunchtime Laughter Club. Recently Dr. Madan Kataria, founder and president of Laughter Club International, was visiting the United States from India and spoke on TV about the Laughter Clubs, which are very popular with businesspeople. (You can find more information on his Web site: www.worldlaughtertour.com). In December of 1999 an All-India Laughter Convention was held, featuring, among other items, an Inter Club Exchange Program where laughter club members from one city invite and provide home stay to ten delegates from a laughter club of another city on reciprocal basis, to build goodwill and brother/sisterhood through laughter. Their mission is good health and world peace through laughter. They strongly believe in the power of some good laughing time before they start their day's work.

Perhaps at your office a few minutes of laughter could be used to start meetings. It would release a lot of tension and foster good relations, creativity, and productivity.

3 ✦ Frogs Jumping from Lily Pads: Becoming a Witness to the Mind

YOUR SOLE CONCERN SHOULD BE, AS THOUGHT SUCCEEDS THOUGHT, TO AVOID CLINGING TO ANY OF THEM.

—HUANG PO

A man came to the Japanese Zen master Ikkyo and asked him for some words of wisdom to guide him in life. Ikkyo nodded agreeably and wrote on a piece of paper the word "attention." The man said he could not understand and asked for something more. Ikkyo wrote, "attention, attention." After a further request for an explanation, Ikkyo wrote his final statement for the man. "Attention, attention, attention means attention."

The special knack of meditation is to develop the one who pays attention, the watcher. When we do a simple sitting meditation, we sit comfortably with our eyes closed and just begin to watch the energies that move within us all the time: thoughts, sensations, emotions. We develop the knack of simply watching these distractions go by with a feeling of acceptance.

How do we acquire this knack? We begin by being a witness to the mind, by becoming separate from the mind.

If you watch a dog, you are clearly not the dog; if you look at a tree, you are separate from the tree. The same applies to the mind. Watching is the key. Watch the mind, without repressing, without preventing, without judging, and slowly you will begin to *disidentify,* realizing that you are not your thoughts, sensations, emotions.

I like to use the image of a frog on a lily pad. When a frog is on a lily pad, resting but ready to move, it is totally alert and awake, yet its body is relaxed. The frog is totally present, observing the activity of the pond, waiting for the right moment to jump. It is not in the grip of fearful thoughts, which might take it into the past or the future; nor is it contracted by anxiety, which might impede its ability to jump. It is free.

We attain a similar freedom by watching and disidentifying from our thoughts, sensations, emotions. Once we have acquired the knack, we, too, are relaxed, yet alert and ready to jump with creativity, total presence, and joy.

Simply by watching the disturbance of mind, body, and emotions, with nonjudgment and acceptance, slowly, over time, the traffic of the mind begins to slow down, and we move from being controlled by the mind to connecting with the heart. This brings us more balance and clarity as it accesses our inner intelligence, dignity, and wisdom.

This is what happens in meditation. The meditator takes a journey from the outer realm to the inner, subjective world where she finds the parts of herself she often ignores, forgets about, or is disconnected from: her feelings, emotions, soul, her essential being. Patience is needed, but this knack of witnessing brings rich rewards. It is a thread of awareness we can weave into the fabric of everyday life.

Try this: Move your right hand without any watchfulness. Now move it again, this time watching from *inside* the whole movement. Do you see how different the two movements are? They are just completely and qualitatively different. The first action is mechanical, robotic. The second is conscious. When you are conscious you feel the hand from within. When you are not conscious you only know the hand from without.

It is not that meditation is against the mind; it is beyond the mind. The mind is our bridge from the subconscious to the conscious, our gateway of expression to the outer world. Be grateful for it. Find ways to appreciate the insights, understandings, and creativity it brings. Don't see it as an enemy, but as a friend.

As this friendship with the mind deepens, the mind will no longer disturb you during meditation. You are not fighting it; you are simply letting its thoughts pass by. This is the background, the soil in which the roses of meditation can blossom. If we befriend the mind, allowing it to subside into its natural place in the background, our qualities of relaxation, humor, compassion, awareness, self-acceptance will flower.

Whatever you are doing—walking, sitting, eating—try to do it watchfully. Or if you are not doing anything, just breathing, resting, relaxing in the grass, try to bring yourself to an awareness that you are a watcher. Yes, you will forget, over and over again. You will get involved in some thought, some emotion, some sentiment—anything to distract you from being the watcher. Just remember and come back to your center of watching.

By making this a continuous inner process, you will be surprised how life can change its quality. Once we reach that place of watcher, or witness, we begin to see ourselves with more clarity and objectivity. We see the dramas in our lives

with perspective and compassion, and insights and understandings will begin to arise naturally.

The mind and the ego will want to make it complicated, but
it is not. Mind always wants to control. It is a technician; technology is its field. But watchfulness is beyond its control. It is
beyond it, above it, and in fact can be death to the control the
mind can have over us.

Maria's Story

Maria had come to see me for a meditation counseling session
early one spring evening. She had been attending my meditation classes for several months. When she arrived she was
clearly full of tension, aggression, and frustration from her
workday as a sales rep for a large advertising company. She
resembled a storm cloud ready to burst. I suggested we begin
with fifteen minutes of the Gibberish meditation and then sit
in silence for fifteen minutes. She readily agreed. After releasing the pent-up volumes of mental, physical, and emotional
stress through the Gibberish meditation, we both sat down,
closed our eyes, and watched what was happening on the
inside. Simply watching the thoughts of the mind pass by, the
coming and going of emotions, sensations in the body, our
bodies relaxed and we fell into a profound silence.

Afterward, when we began to discuss meditation, Maria suddenly burst out laughing. Several moments passed before
Maria could begin to discuss the meditation with me. She was
laughing at herself. During the silence of the watching she had
become aware of how much stress she created for herself with
her hectic lifestyle. She saw how her mind kept pushing her on
a grueling schedule, constantly filling her with anxiety about

making more sales, keeping up with her monthly quota, keeping "in" with her boss. She had every evening jam-packed with social events: tickets for a play, dinner, a computer class. She lived at a manic pace and was constantly exhausted and stressed out.

In those magical moments she saw the funny side of it, with so much tension released from her body and mind, she was no longer so "involved" in it. The watching had helped her to *disidentify* from the stream of commands issuing from her mind. She was able to take a step back and review her work week objectively and see how crazy making it was. She was so relieved by the insights that she burst out laughing, which of course released even more tension. She had come to understand that she was not her mind. She could take back control of her life. By creating a space for meditation she learned to see what the mind was doing. She was eventually able to let go of some of her stress-creating habits and freed up more of her time for relaxation and enjoyment.

Don't Fight, Just Watch

When you try to meditate, and especially at first, thoughts will come; they will surround you from everywhere. They will be like clouds; even the little bit of blue sky will be lost. They will buzz like a swarm of bees stopping us from seeing clearly. And when there are too many thoughts, the natural instinct is to fight with them.

Try fighting with your own shadow. You will be defeated, not because the shadow is so powerful but because the shadow is *not*. And how can you win in a fight against something that is not? Thoughts are shadows. If you try to fight them you will be defeated.

> *To glimpse that truth within yourself,*
> *For even just a moment is worth*
> *More than all heavens, all worlds.*
>
> —RUMI

You have to remain a watcher, a witness. Just watch the thoughts, absolutely calm and quiet; watch. Let them come, let them go, let them arise, let them disappear. Simply take note: the thought is arising, the thought is there, the thought is gone—and some day you will start to notice the gap in between the thoughts. Over time the thoughts will become smaller, and the gap will become bigger.

Listening to music can help us understand this process of watching and becoming aware of the gaps in between the words. Between each musical note there is a gap of silence. It is this silence that distinguishes one note from another, in the same way that between each thought there is a gap of silence. As the world-renowned cellist Pablo Casals said: "The most important thing in music is what is *not* the notes."

Try listening to some music that is not overcrowded with notes. I particularly like *Zenotes* by Shastro and Nadama (information on ordering this CD can be found on page 194). Sit down and close your eyes. As you listen to the music, notice the notes and bring your awareness to the gaps in between the notes. You will find this deeply relaxing, and it will invite you to be more aware of your own inner silence.

The liberation you feel once you realize that you are not the mind can be extraordinary. There is no more anxiety; you are at ease, in a deep let go. You know you can drop down beyond the mind to your inner haven of peace and stillness.

Be Aware of What You Put into Your Mind

Remember, too, to think about what you put into your mind. A year before Y2K a friend of mine kept telling me what a catastrophe he thought it was going to be. The reality was not at all what he had imagined. Allowing the thought in, the mind lives in all this anxiety. You can choose not to feed it.

I don't mean be an ostrich with your head in the sand, disconnected from reality. Keep a balance, remembering to feed your mind with beauty. Then when you are watching the mind in meditation at least you are watching more positive thoughts.

Think about decorating your mind the way you would your body. You keep your body clean; you keep it fresh with sweet-smelling fragrances because you want your body to be loved and respected by others. In a similar way, decorate your mind with great art, poetry, music, literature. Then it will have a music and a poetry of its own. And it will be easier to transcend.

For example, the ninteenth-century English poet William Wordsworth fills his mind with a vision of daffodils in his poem "I Wandered Lonely As a Cloud." Later on, this pleasure is renewed when he is in a meditative frame of mind:

> *A host, of golden daffodils;*
> *Beside the lake, beneath the trees,*
> *Fluttering and dancing in the breeze.*
>
> *Continuous as the stars that shine*
> *And twinkle on the milky way,*
> *They stretched in never-ending line*
> *Along the margin of a bay:*

Ten thousand saw I at a glance,
Tossing their heads in sprightly dance. . . .

For oft, when on my couch I lie
In vacant or in pensive mood,
They flash upon that inward eye
Which is the bliss of solitude;
And then my heart with pleasure fills,
And dances with the daffodils.

WITNESSING MEDITATIONS

The following techniques are great for helping develop the qualities of the watcher. They include the more advanced, classic "sitting still" technique Vipassana. You can also try the Gibberish (page 41), Osho Dynamic (page 44), Laughter (page 63), and Mystic Rose (page 149) meditations, which will help to unburden some of the mental overload so that you are freer to enjoy the present moment.

Thirty-Second Stop Technique

The benefit of this technique is that it can almost instantly bring you to awareness and help you relax. By practicing this technique regularly, by and by a subtle relaxed alertness will begin to weave itself into your day. Just knowing that you can access this state of relaxation at any time will help you feel more in control of your life, more in touch with yourself. It's a great tool for giving yourself some temporary respite in the midst of your busy days.

It's quite simple. Whenever you're feeling stressed, whatever you're doing—walking along the street, folding laundry, engaged in

some activity in your office—stop. Yes, stop completely, no movement. Freeze frame.

It is so easy to lose ourselves in all the activities of our day. The
point of this technique is to help us remember. If you can suddenly
say, "Stop!" and the body stops totally, the mind, because it is taken
unaware, will also stop. And for those split seconds, with the mind
stopped in its tracks, you will penetrate at rocket speed to your center. It is miraculous, really. And by and by, as you get in the habit of
stopping to remember yourself, you will have clearer and clearer
glimpses of your center.

For thirty seconds just be present with whatever is happening.
Are you breathing? How is your body? Where is the mind? Where
are you? In the present? The past? The future? Watch, observe, notice
yourself, without judgment. Then start moving again.

You can try this technique by yourself or with a friend. You might
ask your friend to surprise you with a thirty-second stop when
you're walking down the street. Or you can try it yourself anytime—
at work, on the bus, in the grocery store, in an elevator, doing the
dishes. But remember it must be done suddenly.

Try not to think about it ahead of time; try not to think, Now I'm
going to go to my center and something miraculous is going to happen. This kind of sudden shift is not something you can plan. Simply
stop suddenly, wait, come into the present, and see what comes.

Vipassana

One of the best techniques for becoming a witness to the mind is
Vipassana. Vipassana is a traditional Buddhist meditation, developed
by Gautama The Buddha, 2,500 years ago, in which the meditator
sits with eyes closed, focusing awareness on the breathing—on the
flow of air in and out of the nose, or on the rise and fall of the
belly—and simply watches whatever might arise.

Vipassana practice allows us to see the true nature of reality as a constantly changing process and in so doing, one begins to accept all aspects of life—pleasure and pain, fear and joy—with increasing equanimity. Grounded in the present moment, balanced awareness leads us to a deep stillness that can give us a growing understanding of the nature of life. From this insight, wisdom and compassion become truly possible.

A simple one-hour practice I like very much has two stages: Stage one involves sitting silently for forty-five minutes; stage two involves Zen walking for fifteen minutes. You can start out with ten or fifteen minutes of sitting and several minutes of walking, then slowly increase the time to one hour as you get used to it. If you cannot sit still, then do one of the Moving meditations first, or go running, jogging, or exercising at the gym, and then sit.

STAGE ONE: *Sitting*

Find a place to sit. It doesn't have to be a silent place. Experiment until you find the situation you feel most relaxed in. A chair might help, or a meditation bench or any arrangement of cushions. Sit with your back and head straight but not rigid, eyes closed, and the body as still as possible. If you need to move a part of the body during the sitting, do so slowly and with awareness, saying to yourself, "Right now I am moving my arm" or "right now I am stretching out my legs." (Remember that meditation is not about getting it right or wrong; it is not about torture but awareness of whatever is happening.)

Vipassana can actually be done three ways. Try them all or choose the one that suits you best.

The first Vipassana technique involves awareness of your actions, your body, your mind, your heart. The Buddha has said there are three classic ways of suffering: by clinging, by rejecting, or by wanting clarity when the mind is confused. This practice teaches us acceptance.

As you sit silently, if your leg begins to ache, move it to a more comfortable position with awareness, knowing perfectly that you are moving your leg in that moment. Whatever thoughts are passing across the screen of the mind, just be a watcher. Don't cling or reject; accept. Whatever emotions pass by on the screen of your heart, just remain a witness—don't get involved, don't get identified, don't evaluate what is good, what is bad. Simply dwell in a state of alert, wakeful attention, which clings to no content and is not directed toward any object.

The idea here is to reach a choiceless awareness. Just be a witness, like a scientist observing data, with no judgment. Instead of thinking, "I am sad," say to yourself, "there is sadness around me, there is joy around me." Just watch the emotion or mood. You are a watcher on the hills, and everything else is going on in the valley. Watch whatever comes up as clouds passing in the sky; neither cling nor reject.

The second practice involves becoming aware of your breathing. There is no special breathing technique; ordinary, natural breathing is fine. As you inhale, your belly naturally rises up, and as you exhale, your belly settles down again. Become aware of the belly, its rising and falling. Just the very awareness of the belly rising and falling . . . it is really the life energy, the spring of life that is rising up and falling down with each breath.

As you become more aware of the belly, the mind naturally quiets, the heart becomes silent, and moods disappear. While the first technique involves three steps, becoming aware of your body, your mind and your emotions, your moods, this technique is a single step and you may find it easier. Just feel the belly moving up and down. Women often prefer this one.

The third technique involves awareness of the breath passing through the nostrils. Unlike the belly breathing technique, which brings warmth, this technique brings a certain coolness. Men often prefer it; it's a feeling they are more familiar with. Just feel the breath going in through the nostrils and coming out, going in, coming out. . . .

Once you've tried all three techniques, you may find that you prefer one or that you like to do two together. Or you might even like a combination of the three. Whatever feels easy. Remember, easy is right.

STAGE TWO: *Zen Walking*

You'll want to follow stage one, sitting, by spending fifteen minutes doing Zen walking. This stage involves slow, ordinary walking based on the awareness of your feet touching the ground. While you walk, your attention should go to the contact each foot makes with the ground (or floor). Keep your eyes lowered so that you can only see the ground a few steps ahead. Be alert to the movements of your body.

As you settle into this meditation, the mind will quiet and the ego will disappear. You will still be there, of course, but with no feeling of "I." You will have opened the doors and now you wait, with your loving, trusting heart for the moment of silence, of joy, of serenity to arise.

Remember not to be too serious. Nothing special is supposed to happen. There is nothing to figure out or analyze, no success or failure. You are simply allowing yourself to be less identified with the body, mind, emotions, and environment, which then leaves space for insight or understanding to arise.

Remember, *let the mind pass by.* These are the five key words for watching the mind. There is no concentration, because concentration creates tension. No forcing, no trying to stop the mind, no fighting with the mind. Just let the traffic of the mind pass by. You are the watcher, observing, disidentified, with no judgment, accepting whatever passes by, as if one would sit high up on a mountaintop, watching life pass by with no attachment or involvement. This will bring you to your essential self.

Simple Reminders

Here are a few tips to help you cultivate the qualities of the watcher and reduce the noise in your daily life. You might also like to try my CD *Witnessing the Mind* (information for ordering the CD can be found on page 194).

1 ✦ *Avoid watching scary movies or TV programs.*

The mind is already filled with fears. You don't want to shovel more coals into that furnace. Choose instead stories that are heartwarming, inspiring, uplifting, humorous.

2 ✦ *Walk two blocks down the street remembering yourself.*

Remember to be the watcher, observing your thoughts, with no judgment. There is a story that Ouspensky, a disciple of the Russian mystic Gurdjieff, tried to do this. He was shocked to realize that he couldn't even walk two blocks without getting caught up in his mind. But keep trying it; it gets easier over time.

3 ✦ *Imagine yourself to be a mountain.*

See yourself as calm, centered, disidentified from the changing weather that swirls around you. It might be stormy, sunny and clear, freezing cold, or torrential rain. The mountain remains unmoved, untouched, stable, grounded in itself.

4 ✦ *Observe the mind as you would a TV screen.*

Watch the different shows your mind flashes across the screen and remember you are the watcher, disidentified, relaxed. You are the master, in control, calm, centered, viewing everything with objectivity and clarity.

5 ✦ *Practice the art of doing nothing.*

The art of sitting silently, doing nothing, simply watching, is the essence of meditation. But doing nothing is not as easy as one may suppose. When working hard at the office, although we may fondly daydream of lazing idly around, for most of us the desire for inactivity doesn't usually last long. We tend to get bored, restless, fidgety, needing something to do. We reach to flip on the television, go to a football game, garden, jump on our bike for a ride, head to the movies, call our friends, chitchat over tea or coffee.

It seems that our idea of leisure is a highly active one, as if the last thing we really want to do is absolutely nothing. This is because when the outer activity ceases, the inner activity begins to rise to the surface of our consciousness. Sitting doing nothing, we don't usually experience silence and peace. Instead, we are surprised and disappointed by how busy and noisy it is inside our own heads. We are puzzled; we think that there have never been so many thoughts in our mind as there are now. These thoughts have always been there; it is just that we have never been aware of them. We have to come to terms with this inner rush hour of thoughts.

See if you can find the time to do nothing every day. Try it for five minutes to start and just witness the busyness of your mind.

4 ✦ Apples and Oranges:
Practicing Nonjudgment

A mother is standing in a long line for the checkout counter in a busy supermarket. Her five-year-old daughter is having trouble waiting in line. She is acting out, bothering other people, especially a fragile old lady. She keeps repeating the few lines of a song she has just learned, jumping up and down, running in circles around the shopping cart, and generally getting in people's way. The mother patiently stands behind her cart, not saying anything to her child about her behavior.

The woman standing in front of them in line is getting more and more irritated and finally turns to the mother and says angrily, "How can you allow your child to behave like this? Aren't you going to say anything to her?"

The mother replies, "Her father just died. She's already going through so much. The grief counselor told me that she might act out her anger at her loss for a while until she comes to accept it."

The woman in line realizes that she has been quick to judge

without knowing the whole story. She immediately feels her heart fill with compassion for the girl and her mother and wants to know if there is anything she can do for them.

Her angry judgments are transformed into compassion when she discovers the whole truth of the situation.

Like the angry shopper, we all make these kinds of judgments over the course of our busy days. When we see someone scowling or pushing his way onto the elevator or driving too fast, we want to label and categorize: This is good, that is bad; this is okay, that is not okay. The mind is juvenile, hasty, eager to jump in and judge. But we don't know what's causing other people's behavior, do we? Maybe they are on their way to their father's funeral or to the hospital emergency room where their daughter has just been taken after an accident. *We don't know.*

As we practice watching the mind in meditation, we begin to observe our judgments. When they arise, we can accept them and let them go. Nonjudgment means accepting life the way it is, getting beyond the good/bad duality of the mind to a place of relaxation and inner stillness.

When we judge we cut ourselves off from the world around us; we lose our sensitivity, we shrink, we close. Through the practice of watching, by and by a subtle awareness arises that keeps us open-minded for unknown possibilities to emerge. We become more available for life to happen through us. We become more loving.

Mind moves horizontally from one moment to the next, like a railway train with many compartments. It wants to put every person and situation into a compartment. When we suspend judgment, we can get off the train and *participate* in life; have a cup of tea, joke with the ticket collector, go for a bicycle ride, smell the fragrance of a rose flower, sit in a leafy sanctuary, and listen to the song of a lark high in the sky.

Life is always original, new. It is vertical. Each moment can rise into height or fall into depth. It is an ongoing process, like a river flowing toward the ocean. Consciousness is also vertical. There is no past or future. Every moment is new in existence. Either you enjoy it or you miss it. When you watch a sunset, every evening it is always new. It is never the same as the night before. Try it. Watch the sunset every night for seven days. Each night existence will give you an original sunset.

When we judge we become more identified with the horizontal, with the train, putting people, events, situations into compartments. It is a habit. The moment something is there we judge it. This is a beautiful flower; that is an ugly house. To judge, the past is needed. To say, this face is beautiful, we must have something to compare it with, some vague notion from the past, some accumulated sense of what a beautiful face is.

When we don't bring in the past, when, for example, we look at someone's face and don't come from the mind, when we simply look, we participate deeply with this face, this person, this mystery, here and now. In this moment, the person is neither ugly nor beautiful; all judgments disappear. No more good/bad, fat/thin, short/tall. There is just meeting, just merging of energies. Participation. This is nonjudgment.

As Heraclitus said, "You can't step in the same river twice." In the same way, you can't meet the same person twice because we are like a river, continuously flowing. We never know what will happen.

Look at a flower with no judgment and suddenly the heart of the flower will be open to you. It will invite you to participate with it in the joy of existence. As the English poet William Blake says, "Energy is delight. There is no other delight. The very vitality, the very energy of being, is delight, is bliss."

Try this exercise: Sit facing a friend. Close your eyes, both of you. Sit and wait and only open your eyes and look into the face of your friend when you can do so with no judgment. Sit and wait until your heart is filled with so much love for your friend that all judgment, good or bad, disappears, until just a feeling of pure beingness with your friend emerges. Move into the feeling of participation, feel the mystery that is your friend, become aware of everything that you don't know about your friend, bring awareness to the joy of your friendship, the joy of sharing these moments. This energy between you is delight.

Judging and comparing do have their uses. When we are shopping for a home mortgage, or buying a new car or a breakfast cereal, the mind's ability to judge and compare can come in very handy. But human beings aren't cars or homes. We cannot package ourselves up and compare deals.

How can you compare a rose with a tulip? Or judge a poplar tree for not being more like an oak? Just because some of us prefer eating mango rather than pineapple doesn't mean there is anything wrong with the poor pineapple. It's simply different. Just because some of us are shy or tall or round or Jewish or Asian or right-handed or freckle-faced does not make any of us better than another. The more people are accepted for who they are, the more they bloom. As the British aristocrat Dame Edith Sitwell said, "If one is a greyhound, why try to look like a Pekingese?"

We not only affect others with our judgments, we are affected by their judgments as well. Women in our society, for example, know that we are supposed to look a certain way. Thin. We are judged for the work we do. It is more prestigious to be a lawyer than a cook, or a financial planner than a garbage disposal worker. And we internalize these judgments.

As the years pass we often tend to be more and more critical and judgmental of ourselves. This continual self-judgment has the same effect as continual judgment by others. We feel bad, we contract, and we are fearful.

Susan's Story

Susan became obsessed with being thin because her boyfriend remarked once about her waistline looking a bit filled out. She took his judgment of her waistline as an indication that there was something wrong with her and was desperate to put it right. Through her practice of meditation, observing the judgments of the mind, learning to disidentify from them, she was able to start to see herself with more love and compassion. The punishing dieting and exercising she was doing to reduce her waistline were creating stress in her body, which she was able to gain insight and understanding about. She realized that by freeing herself from the effect of judgment, she could love herself and accept that her boyfriend loved her, too, with or without a tiny waist. His remark did not mean that he didn't love her, or that she couldn't love herself. She could let it pass by.

We are afraid of the insanity of the mind. We are afraid of being lonely. The more we stay with it, watching with no judgment, accepting, welcoming, one day the loneliness will suddenly disappear into an unexpected state of aloneness. Or "all-one-ness." That space where there is nothing to prove, and nothing to do. That space of silence, peace, and serenity.

The thirteenth-century Persian poet Rumi invites us to embrace all that comes our way and use it as a means to discover ourselves.

> *Every morning a new arrival . . .*
> *A joy, a depression, a meanness. . . .*
> *Welcome and entertain them all!*

Karen's Story

Karen wanted to be a singer for as long as she could remember. As a child she liked to sing and hum to herself as she played. She had four older brothers who laughed at her when she sang because they were only interested in rough and tumble boys' games and called her a sissy. Over the years, Karen stopped singing.

When she came to see me, she was working in an insurance office dealing with claims. She wasn't happy with her life. As Karen learned meditation and practiced watching the judgments of the mind, she became aware that she was repressing her joy and passion for singing because of painful memories of her brothers' remarks. The effect of their judgments had caused her to shut down her joy of singing for fear of being laughed at. This had also led her to judge herself.

Karen had difficulty accepting herself the way she was and accepting one of her passions in life, which was to sing. Why is this the case for so many of us? Why is it so difficult for us to accept ourselves the way we are? There are two reasons. First we often learn plenty about what is wrong with us, as Karen did, but very little about what is right with us. So we grow up feeling insecure, inadequate, and fearful, wondering if we will ever be okay. Through meditation, we can put a halt to this stream of criticism and judgment and reclaim ourselves. By observing judgments passing across the mind we can learn to adopt an attitude of nonjudgment toward ourselves.

But there is still another part to this answer. We are all born with a potential to fulfill, whether it is to be an interior designer, a cook, a software engineer, an artist, or a poet. And until we are on our path, heading in the direction of fulfilling our creative potential, we will be dissatisfied with ourselves. As Karen rediscovered her passion for singing, she found a far greater acceptance and contentment with herself and her life.

Deep down our souls will be discontented until we start moving in the direction of what gives passion and meaning to our lives. Once again, meditation can be a powerful part of this self-discovery process.

NONJUDGMENT MEDITATIONS

You can do these for as little as a few minutes or for five, ten, or fifteen minutes or longer. It might make it more fun to try some of these with a friend, remembering of course not to compare, but simply as an awareness exercise done with love and compassion for yourselves.

Left-handed Painting

Here's a great nonjudgment technique I teach in my meditation workshops. Everyone gets paper and paints and fifteen minutes to paint a picture of anything they feel like painting. They use their left hand if they are right-handed and their right hand if they are left-handed. Then they walk around in silence looking at all the pictures. I am always amazed at how fast and furious the judgments come racing into my mind. A setting like this provides a valuable opportunity to simply watch them, accept them, and let them pass by.

You could try this yourself with a few friends or by going to a museum or gallery. You could even try this in a shoe store, or a boat harbor, or by driving around looking at houses. Just notice the judgments going on inside your head. Try not to judge yourself for judging. Simply observe how many judgments the mind keeps on making, nonstop, about what it sees. See if you can observe the paintings without judgment, simply participating with the painting in that moment, observing exactly what's in front of your eyes.

This can help you to become disidentified from the judgments. Your view will be less distorted. You can then see the person or object in front of you with more objectivity and clarity, and with more love.

Walking Down the Street

Next time you're walking down a street, or sitting on a park bench or in a coffee shop, notice how you judge people as they pass by; for example, the way they dress; whether they smoke, are overweight, are chewing gum; how loud they talk, what kind of car they drive. Bring your attention inward, to observing your mind and the judgments it is making on what it sees. The knack of it is to bring our attention from the people outside of us, to ourselves, and what is going on inside of us. For example, as you walk down the street, first bring your attention to yourself, to your feet on the ground, your breathing, the swing of your arms. Become aware that "in this moment I am walking down the street." And now, observing the passersby, notice any judgments passing across your mind. It is a shift of perspective that will bring you more in touch with yourself.

Someone Else's Shoes

Whenever you find yourself judging someone, take a moment to see if you can imagine what might be happening in *their* lives. Maybe they've just lost a loved one, or are having problems with their marriage, or are under financial stress. Maybe they are trying to quit smoking and the one cigarette you see them smoking is actually the first one they've had all week and in fact represents great progress in their effort to quit.

The mind has a narrow view; it only sees one piece of the picture. We conjure up stories about people all the time without knowing their reality much at all. See if you can shift your perspective to a place of not knowing, because the truth is we don't ever fully know what's going on with other people. By opening our minds and widening our perspective, we can open the doorway to a place of compassionate nonjudgment.

Try to keep an open mind. Participate with people in *this* moment and a much deeper enjoyment of life will come to you.

Looking Without Judging

Judgment clouds our sight; it's like looking at a view through a dirty window. This technique gets us comfortable with just looking at things without judgment, allowing us to be present with what is.

Try just looking at a flower or some other small thing for a few minutes. Don't say "beautiful" or "ugly." Don't say anything. Don't bring in words. Simply look. The mind will feel uncomfortable; it would like you to say something. Try to just ride through this feeling. Try to just look.

Start with neutral things, things that don't hold any charge for you: a rock, a flower, a tree, the sun rising, a bird in flight, a cloud moving in the sky. Only when you have gotten used to the technique should you try it with people. As you begin to look at people without judgment, you will see them more clearly and with more compassion.

By opening your vision, your heart, and your mind in this way, you will find a greater flexibility, openness, and receptivity within yourself to the world at large.

Remember, just look, without judgment; just be present with what is.

Simple Reminders

Remember, it is the nature of the mind to judge and compare, and we don't have to feel bad about it. It just is. So watch out for judging yourself for judging! Simply notice, become aware, like a scientist observing data. Then accept the judgments and let them pass by. Don't fight with them, try to hide them, or push them down into the unconscious. This way we create trouble for ourselves. Bring them out into the open, see them, admit to them, and accept them. They will then pass by without clouding your vision.

The point is to bring awareness and compassion to yourself. The benefit is clarity. Learning nonjudgment is like cleaning your glasses so you can see more clearly.

1 ✦ If you find yourself making negative judgments about a person in your life, for example your boss, a coworker, an employee, your mother-in-law, or your spouse, take some quiet time and ask yourself these questions.
   ✦ Am I thinking in ways that tend to be overly negative?
   ✦ Are my expectations realistic?
   ✦ Would an objective observer view or interpret this situation differently?
   ✦ Will this make any difference to me in a week, a month, a year, or ten years?

2 ✦ When judging notice what happens in your body, the sensations and feelings. Do you notice a contraction, a shrinking?

3 ✦ When you observe you are making negative judgments about a person, make a practice of sending them a blessing, of wishing them well. See if you can incorporate that person in your heart, despite what you don't like about them, and see how much better that makes you feel.

As the Chinese mystic Wu-Men said: "If your mind isn't clouded by unnecessary things, this is the best season of your life."

5 ✦ Meditation Is Not Instant Coffee: Developing Patience

ALL BEINGS ARE FROM THE VERY BEGINNING BUDDHAS.

IT IS LIKE WATER AND ICE:

APART FROM WATER, NO ICE,

OUTSIDE LIVING BEINGS,

NO BUDDHAS. . . .

—HAKUIN EKAKU
Japanese Zen master

These are lines of a poem by the Japanese Zen master Hakuin Ekaku called "Song of Meditation." Mystics down the ages have been telling us this, that we are already buddhas, but we don't believe them. What, me, a buddha? No way. When we are knee deep in life's stresses, how can we possibly be buddhas?

Meditation can help us remember our buddha nature. When we meditate, we create a space and invite this quality to come. It takes time and requires patience. It cannot be forced, faxed, e-mailed. Nor can it be overnight expressed. But if we wait patiently, given enough encouragement the guest will surely come. This is a certainty, because what we are waiting for is not somewhere on the outside, but inside us, waiting for us to reconnect with it. It is just a matter of time.

At the beginning, all this patient waiting and inviting might seem difficult. This is because we are in the habit of getting what we want instantly like a cup of instant coffee. With meditation it is very important that you not be in a hurry. Choose techniques that you enjoy (it's just human nature that we won't keep at something that we don't enjoy) and stick with it. Many people feel like failures when they first start to meditate. That's very natural. Don't despair. Meditation is only difficult at first. It becomes easier and easier as you continue.

We must remember that for our whole lives our attention has been focused outward, not inward. We don't know how to come in toward ourselves; it is not our habit. So at first we are bound to fail. It takes a big shift of attention to start traveling inward.

But in time, with your continued practice, it will happen. Don't compare with anyone else; everyone will go at a different pace. We have all read different books, been exposed to different religions, different people, and we all have different skills. We come from different cultures, education, family background. There are a thousand and one differences between us and others. So how can we compare? What is needed is patient, silent work. It comes gradually. So don't rush it.

> Each grass and each form itself is the entire earth . . .
> Each moment is all being, is the entire world. Reflect now whether any being or any world is left out of the present moment.
>
> —DOGEN
> *thirteenth-century Japanese Zen master*

Try this little technique right now.

Close your eyes and be in the present moment, this moment, which is now. Is what Dogen says true?

Persist

Meditation requires persistence.

When I started my own business, all my impatience came up—"why is it taking so long to get going?" and so on. With the advance of technology we have gotten used to having everything instantaneously. Microwave dinners, cell phones, the Internet—it's all about speed. They say it takes about five years to get a new business off the ground. When you start out, you have to nurture it and stay with it even when it feels like it's not happening. You may put a lot out at the beginning and nothing comes back, or very little. You just have to keep going and trusting.

Meditation is similar. I'm not saying it will take five years to master; I'm saying the process is the same. You keep at it and slowly, slowly over time, the benefits will begin to appear.

The old adage "if at first you don't succeed, then try and try again" fits well here. I remember my first attempts to make lemon meringue pie. The results were dreadful. But after several attempts I succeeded. Persist in your meditation and you *will* get the results you are after.

Practice

Spending time with children can be very helpful. I know that being a mother slowed me down and brought me into the here and now in a very powerful way. You can't hurry a baby or a small child; he has his own rhythm and pace. Or you can try, but you will create problems if you do.

Children can watch a snail for a full half-hour, entranced with its progress, or watch the activities in a small pond, enraptured for hours by the fish, plants, and little critters and birds who visit. They have a far greater ability than we do to be in the present and not be in a rush.

Have you ever spent thirty minutes watching a butterfly, or a procession of ants or the birds in the sky? Try it. It slows you right down and forces a certain patience.

I remember going out to dinner with my son Paul one evening when he was about eight or nine. The conversation somehow got onto the topic of tomato ketchup: the different brands, tastes, textures, shapes of the bottles, glass or plastic, screw-on caps or flip-off tops. Paul was a real aficionado of ketchup and was just delighted with the discussion, totally absorbed. I was enjoying our outing, but I was also aware that a part of my restless speedy mind just wished he would hurry up and grow up so we could have conversations about more "important" topics. In that moment I saw that I, the great meditator, was the one who was missing out, not my son. The speedy mind, by being in such a hurry, was wanting to rush my son through his childhood.

Children can be great teachers for us; I certainly learned something from my son that day. After all, what matters more? The topic of the dinner conversation or the quality of the interaction?

Through meditation we can also rediscover our own childlike qualities, our ability to be patient and present. (I particularly recommend the Mystic Rose [see page 149] technique for this.)

The mind is a doer and likes to be busy. It is the yang, the masculine side of us, the left brain, whereas meditation comes from our receptive, yin, feminine side, the right brain. The mind and the ego might like to practice all kinds of ascetic techniques, fasts, vows, and denials and gather all kinds of knowledge. The mind thinks that the more it does, the more quickly it will attain "enlightenment." The more knowledge it has, the quicker meditation will come.

The mind thinks this way because this is how our society functions. Everything is accomplished by going through a linear progression of steps. This will not work for meditation. A reversal is needed. Let go. Do your meditation techniques with a spirit of play, of no expectation. As you continue to meditate, your heart will become more aware, loving, sensitive, and alert. Your being will start seeing things you had not seen before. You will discover new spaces within yourself. Something new will happen every day, every moment.

Your meditations are like a bath or a shower. They give you a freshness. But this freshness is not your enlightenment. It simply prepares the way. You must never reach to enlightenment. It is always the other way around—enlightenment reaches to you.

MEDITATIONS FOR DEVELOPING PATIENCE

Our society seems addicted to speed. Faster, like more and louder, is supposed to be better. We try to do too much, and consume more, and the result is overstimulation and exhaustion. Why are we in such a hurry? Where are we going? In our culture, doing is valued over being. We don't like anything slow; waiting makes us impatient. We ignore seasonal cycles that would slow us down; we try to maintain spring's faster pace even in winter. Speed is important in an emergency, and it feels good to run a race. But slowing down our nonemergency actions is an easy way to help us relax and be patient.

Here are a few meditations that are particularly good for developing patience.

Sit Silently and Wait

A meditative awareness comes like a whisper, not a shout, with noiseless footsteps. If you are full of occupations, busyness, and noise it might come and wait, but then it will leave. I can't overstate the importance of having silent, waiting time.

So set aside some time—ten, fifteen, thirty minutes or longer—preferably every day, for sitting in silence. It doesn't matter where you are, just sit, close your eyes, and wait. Don't do anything; just sit in great waiting with an open, trusting heart. Then if something is to "happen" you will be ready to receive it. If nothing happens, at least you've had this "down time" to do nothing, and lord knows we all need that! No matter what, after sitting silently for a while you will feel more in touch with yourself, more peaceful.

Most people find that it works best to do this at the same time every day. It doesn't matter what time you choose, but setting aside a set time, say as a mid-morning break or during your lunch hour, helps make it part of your daily routine. When the inner consciousness knows that the outer consciousness is waiting for it, there is a greater possibility of a meeting.

As you practice doing nothing, by and by an understanding will start to arise between you and the meditative state. As this understanding grows you will start to feel a subtle quality of relaxation, of serenity permeating your whole day.

Just Ordinary Tea

In Japan, the tea ceremony is a Zen tradition that dates back thousands of years. It helps bring a sense of reverence and happiness and joy in the simplicity of the ordinary. Try this simple practice to bring awareness to the ordinary activity of drinking tea. The tea-making process is a great patience practice.

Prepare the tea cups and the teapot. Listen to the kettle and the sound it makes. Pour the tea, smelling the fragrance, savoring the aroma, then tasting the tea and feeling that deep sense of contentment that comes as the tea's warmth enters your body. Feel thankful that you are alive and in this moment drinking tea. Don't think about the past or the future. Surrender to the present moment, just you and the tea, as if nothing else exists. It will give you a taste of meditation, of the beauty and grace that can be brought to even the simplest acts.

You can do this in the mornings, during the day, or at any time that suits your schedule. Allow fifteen to thirty minutes, longer if you have time.

One of my clients likes to do this meditation when she gets home after her busy workday. She showers and changes into relaxing clothes, turns off the phone, puts the mail aside for later, brews her favorite blend of tea, then sits for thirty minutes on her porch, relaxing and enjoying this personal time that she has reserved just for herself. She finds it an invigorating and regenerating way to begin her evening.

If you happen to be reading this on a sweltering hot day, or live in the desert or a very hot climate, you might like to try this with iced tea. Listen to the chink of the ice as it drops into the glass; enjoy the colors through the glass, the mint, slice of lemon, or cherry you might add for flavor. Enjoy the coolness, the refreshing taste, and feel of the ice cold tea as you sip it through a straw relaxing into the moment.

Eating Meditation

I often take my students by surprise when I suggest that eating can be a meditation. As we've discussed, awareness brought to any act makes it a meditation. And this is no less true of eating.

We have all been taught fixed rules about eating. Perhaps when you were a child, you were forced to clean your plate or to eat foods that you didn't like or that your body didn't want. (Were you a member of the Clean Plate Club? I was.) The fear that you might be reprimanded for not eating what is placed in front of you may still be lurking within you, shutting down the connection with your body's natural wisdom. Not to mention how hard it is to keep up with the latest dietary recommendations: Eggs are out; eggs are okay. Avoid all fats; olive oil is good for you. But the body knows no fixed rules. When you eat according to your heart's desire, according to your body's natural need for proper nourishment, the urge to overeat disappears. Learning to listen to the wisdom of your own body is important. When you eat according to your heart's desire, you will find that you are in sync with your body's natural need for proper nourishment.

This meditation can help you reconnect with this basic body knowing. Your body wisdom will come back because you have only forgotten; the knowledge of what foods are best for you is there in the body waiting to be rediscovered.

Though the mind loves to judge and compare, the mind is not doing the eating; the body is. It doesn't matter what other people are eating. What matters is that your body likes the foods you give it.

Meditate before meals.

Every day, before you take food, meditate for a few moments. Simply close your eyes and go inside to feel what your body needs. Bring awareness to your own being, to what your body feels like eating, what you hanker for. Whatever answer you get is called "humming food"—food that hums to you. Eat as much of the humming food as you want, but stick to what your body told you when you asked. Trust that this food will satisfy you.

You'll be able to tell fairly quickly if you've made a mistake. Your stomach won't be happy, and you will know to stop eating a particular food, or to eat less of it. We all have different body types, and what one person's digestive system likes, another's may not.

Humming foods have an entirely different quality from what I call "beckoning foods." Beckoning foods are those things we desire from the mind, not the stomach. Eating problems arise when we eat beckoning food. TV advertisements, descriptions on restaurant menus, glossy magazine photos, colorful food packages on supermarket shelves all distract us from our humming body. No matter how much of these foods we eat, we do not feel satisfied, because the body has no intrinsic need for them. Feeling unsatisfied, we eat more. If we listen to the food that hums for us, our hunger for beckoning food will disappear. If we eat only humming food, we will be satisfied, because the body desires what it really needs, nothing else.

Make eating your meal a meditation.

There is no hurry; take your time. Smell the food; look at it. Touch your food with closed eyes; experience it in every way. Then take a small bite and chew it slowly. Enjoy each sensation; feel the texture, the flavor in your mouth. Be totally present with what you are eating, rather than doing something else at the same time.

Eat alone.

Close your office door or find a place where you can be alone. Turn off the phone ringer; let the machine take the messages. Put a notice on your door: Gone to Lunch. Close your eyes, relax for a minute or two, bring awareness to your breathing, and feel your feet on the ground. Then unwrap your food and lay it out carefully in front of you, making sure you have everything you need. Eat with intention, slowly, enjoying the tastes and textures, and savor the ingredients of your meal. Don't read or look at documents or the computer screen. Just keep your attention on your food.

Remember to breathe slowly and feel your feet on the ground. Feel the body's satisfaction as it digests the food. Pause when you

change to taking a drink. Slowly bring the cup to your mouth and
feel the liquid satisfying your thirst. Just enjoy the sensual pleasure of
eating and drinking.

When you have finished, pause for a few moments with eyes
closed. Sit and breathe. Feel the sense of satisfaction, well-being, and
comfort that a good meal can bring.

Know when to stop.

One of the keys to eating well is knowing when to stop. Try bringing
your awareness to the stomach and allowing it to choose how
much you eat. You will be delighted at how much better you will
feel.

Simple Reminders

And finally, here are a few suggestions for things you can do in
your daily life to help you slow down and practice patience:

1 ✦ Spend more time observing plants, flowers, butterflies,
snails, and other natural phenomena such as stones,
rivers, mountains.

2 ✦ Meander, saunter, or walk directly on the ground.

3 ✦ Get out of your car and ride a bike or a horse.

4 ✦ Engage in "slow" activities such as fishing, bird-watching,
tai chi, meditation.

5 ✦ Sit on porches, benches, or in parks and observe what
goes by.

6 ✦ Lie on the ground and look up at the sky, clouds, or stars.

7 ✦ Take a long, warm bath.

8 ✦ Take time off, do nothing, and "waste" time.

9 ✦ Say "no" to more things.

10 ✦ Turn everything off for a day, an hour, five minutes. No
    phone. No computer. Unplug.
11 ✦ Spend time with children and babies.

These activities help to bring us into balance. They support
our practice of meditation. They invite our inner stillness. They
bring out the Buddha within us.

See if you can commit to trying one or more of these practices on a daily basis. Experiment with the ideas. You might have
more ideas of your own. In this way you will be supporting
your meditation practice, giving encouragement to that inner
space of peace and calm to become easily available to you.

6 ✦ Sailing Uncharted Seas: Discovering Trust

JUST TRUST YOURSELF THEN YOU WILL KNOW HOW TO LIVE.

—GOETHE

There is an old Sufi story. A man has just gotten married and he is coming home with his wife. They are crossing a lake in a boat and suddenly a storm arises. The man is a warrior but the woman becomes very afraid. Life seems to be finished. Any moment they are going to drown. But the man sits silently, calm and quiet, as if nothing is happening.

The woman is trembling with fear and says, "Are you not afraid? Only a miracle can save us. We'll never reach to the other shore. It looks like death is certain. Why aren't you afraid, are you mad? Are you a stone or something?"

The man laughs and takes the sword out of its sheath. The woman becomes even more puzzled. What is he doing? He brings the naked sword close to the woman's neck—so close that it is almost touching her neck. He says, "Are you afraid?" She starts giggling and laughing and says, "Why would I be afraid? If the sword is in your hands, why should I be afraid? I know you love me."

He puts the sword back and says, "This is my answer. I know existence loves us and the sword is in its hands, the storm is in its hands, so whatever happens is going to be good. If we survive, good; if we don't survive, good, because everything is in the hands of existence."

Trust is knowing that life loves you, knowing that we were created by love, for love, to love. Babies, children, birds, animals, trees are connected to this security. It is the mind that creates the separation. The mind wants to understand everything. When it takes over, we become fearful. Fear clouds our judgment and creates misery in our lives.

Brian's Story

One of my clients who has been practicing meditation for many years is the vice president of a savings and loan. One day he was telling me about how he goes about the loan approval process. When a client applies for a loan, of course he has to check out their references, paperwork, and so on. However, there comes a point in the process where he has to sit down with himself and decide whether he can trust the person to pay the money back. He closes his eyes and drops down inside. He gets in touch with his heart and listens to his inner voice, or intuition. He knows that there is never any guarantee to get the money back; he has to trust his own inner "knowing" that this person will repay the money.

In twenty years he has never lost money for the bank. He credits his intuitive good judgment of character to his daily meditation practice. He has time to ask himself inner questions about the authenticy and credibilty of his clients. Over the years, through getting to know himself, being in touch with himself, he has learned to trust himself. Because more than trusting the client, it is himself he has to trust. He is the one making the evaluation.

We all have to make decisions in our lives that require at least some measure of trust: When we arrange to meet a friend, we trust that she will show up; when we confide in a friend, a counselor, our accountant, we trust that he will not divulge our personal business to anyone. In these small ways we are using our inner knowing that we can trust the other person. And if he lets us down, we must still go on trusting, because there are many others out there who will prove trustworthy. We must not let one unfortunate incident deter us from trusting others. *Trust resides in us, not in anyone else.*

Fear lives in the mind; trust lives in the heart. The trusting heart can accept the present situation, knowing that things will unfold in their own way. The trusting heart knows that we cannot control the universe. Trust is a mystery. Like love, it is difficult to define, but when experienced, we know what it is.

There are two ways to discover trust. One way is through awareness. Just make a decision to become aware and watch what the mind does. The more you can disidentify from it, the more you will be able to discover the wisdom of your trusting heart. The other way is through love. Trust and love are intrinsically a part of each other, inextricably intertwined. You can find love through trust or you can find trust through love. It is as if love is the circumference and trust is its very center, its soul; love a temple and trust its innermost shrine.

Trust is not about anybody else. It is an intuitive inner "knowing" that we are connected to an inexhaustible source of love, that there is an all-embracing security, integrity, and balance to the order of things. Even when we don't understand what is happening, trust comforts us that at the right time everything will become clear.

Every child is born full of trust. Unfortunately many of us

lose our connection to our trusting heart as we move through childhood into adulthood. Perhaps we were often criticized and began to think that everything that went wrong was our fault. Perhaps we were left alone a lot, or people forgot to feed us or pick us up from school. Perhaps our parents broke a lot of promises, or our father left our mother, or our mother died. As young children, how could we know that these things were not our fault? We learned to be quick to condemn ourselves for real and imagined shortcomings. Our only recourse was to lock up the heart and retreat to the head, where mistrust and fear took hold.

Meditation gives us a wonderful means to recover trust, to recover the inner richness we have lost. The awareness that comes with meditation guides us back from the head to the heart, from logic to love, from fear to trust. It encourages us to dig a little deeper than the surface so that we begin to notice how often we put ourselves down. It rewards us with renewed confidence that we can trust our intuitive knowings, those gut feelings that keep us safe from outer harm and self-destructive impulses. When we bring awareness to loving and accepting ourselves in this moment, right now, we unearth the key that can reopen our trusting heart.

MEDITATIONS FOR DISCOVERING TRUST

Only the heart knows how to find what is precious.
—FYODOR DOSTOYEVSKY

Where do you begin to develop trust? Start with yourself. Start with the present moment where you are. The following are techniques I use for developing a sense of trust. We lose trust when we become disconnected from our hearts. These techniques are particularly good for healing the heart and reconnecting with trust. You might also try the Laughter (page 63), Osho Dynamic (page 44), Gibberish (page 41), and Mystic Rose (page 149) meditations.

The Good in You

There are voices which we hear in solitude, but they grow faint and inaudible as we enter into the world.

—RALPH WALDO EMERSON

Learn to get in touch with the silence within yourself and know that everything in this life has a purpose.

—ELISABETH KUBLER–ROSS

Bring awareness to loving and accepting yourself in this moment right now. Close your eyes and see the good in yourself. If criticisms, judgments arise, let them pass by. Whatever you see grows in you. That is the secret. So focus on the good.

Remind yourself of the things that are good in you: You are a good friend, a good fix-it person; you are adept on the computer. Make a list of the things you are good at. Whenever you become self-critical or untrusting, take out the list and read it. Give the list to a friend and ask him or her to remind you of these qualities. A client of mine told me that as she was cooking dinner one evening she was feeling very down about herself, that she wasn't any good at anything. She sat down to eat with her family and her ten-year-old daughter said, "You're a great cook, Mom." She had temporarily lost her trust in herself and her daughter's remark brought her back to herself.

To choose the bad is easy. It is downhill. Just take your foot off the gas pedal, turn off the engine, and the car will roll downhill. Goodness is uphill. Much energy and effort and awareness are needed. This is how you grow. And it is moment-to-moment work. Each moment the alternatives are there; each moment you have to decide. It is an ongoing process. Whenever your mind is trying to choose between good and bad, always see the good. If, for example, you find yourself thinking, "I'm such a failure, I can never get anything right, I'm a bad person," you can always choose to replace these thoughts with positive thoughts: "I try hard, I do my job well, and I have a good sense of humor."

One of my clients told me that when she started meditating she kept going over the same scenario in her mind about the time when she broke up with her last boyfriend. It took her a while but she learned to catch herself and focus her thoughts on a more positive topic, like where she might meet a new boyfriend.

Remember, the mind has no power of its own. At the most it can give you alternatives, but the choice finally is yours. So always lean toward the good, even if it is difficult in the beginning. The more you choose goodness, the more you will naturally and spontaneously move toward that. By and by, you will no longer have to choose.

To support your journey into trust, remember the steady reassuring rhythm of the natural world, the ebb and flow of tides, the recurring cycle of the four seasons, the monthly phases of the moon, the daily progression of day into night. It envelops us in a blanket of security and contentment, a sense of well-being. We can rest assured, night will become day, sunset will become sunrise, the birds will start singing in the morning and go quiet at night. We have an innnate trust that that will happen. Although we have no legal document that winter will become spring, or that the wild geese will migrate in the fall, we have trust in the rhythm of the universe.

Think about babies. They are happy for no reason. They are connected to that greater rhythm. They don't need a reason. We were born with that same happiness and trust—for no reason. Through meditation we can regain it.

Our adult minds have been trained to deny to us the existence of the heart; to deny that feeling is also a way of knowing. Self-inquiry, our journey into ourselves, requires trust because we are going into the unknown. We are moving away from the conventional and the traditional, away from the crowd. We are going into the open sea and we don't know whether the other shore exists at all. As John Shedd said, "A ship is safe in harbor—but that's not what ships are for." It is a risk. Imagine the trust Christopher Columbus must have had when he set forth from Spain on the Santa Maria. Many thought he would fall off the edge of the world. But he trusted; somehow he "knew" he would find land. Fortunately for us he did.

The intellect knows how to seek and search, but in order for intellect to be transformed into intelligence, the heart must be opened. The intellect has to trust the heart and follow its directions. Intelligence is intellect in tune with the heart. This is the harmony that allows us to move forward in trust, take risks, and allow our authentic selves to unfold.

Humming

Humming is a longer technique designed to open us to trust, to bring us into our inner sanctuary of peace and serenity. The humming technique has ancient roots in the East. As we hum we are generating our own energy to heal and center ourselves. Humming brings us straight down from the head and into the body, keeping us alert yet relaxed. It has a soothing, calming effect as the vibration of the sounds resonates throughout the body/mind.

Mitchell L. Gaynor, M.D., one of New York's most prominent oncologists and director of Medical Oncology and Integrative Medicine at the Strang-Cornell Cancer Prevention Center, has used the incredible healing power of sound in his clinic and shown how it can dramatically improve health, reduce pain and stress, and awaken creativity. He has even had patients go into cancer remission after using healing sounds.

In his book *The Sounds of Healing,* Gaynor also cites Dr. David Simon, medical director of Neurological Services at Sharp Cabrillo Hospital in San Diego, California, and medical director of the Chopra Center for Well-Being, who has seen that healing chants and music have "measurable physiologic effects." Simon points out that chants are actually metabolized into natural painkillers, releasing healing agents in the body.

The humming technique I like to use is called "Nadabrahma." Nadabrahma is an old Tibetan technique, updated by Osho. It is particularly good for healing the heart on both emotional and physical levels, for releasing emotional distress, and for bringing us to a balanced state of deeply centered well-being. It is also helpful for anyone who suffers from throat, bronchial, lung, and chest problems or has communication difficulties, and is ideal for singers or speakers or anyone who wants to become one.

I also recommend Osho Nadabrahma for anyone who wants to do an active technique but whose state of health is not suitable for the more energetic and cathartic methods. You might like this method simply as a means of becoming more centered and relaxed. It is also great for recharging your batteries when you're running on empty.

You can do Osho Nadabrahma at any time of day, either alone or with others. You will need about an hour and a quarter for it: approximately an hour for the meditation and, very important, fifteen minutes afterward for remaining at rest.

I suggest that you try it for at least a week at the same time of day every day and see how you resonate with it. Many people find it deeply centering and calming, especially if you are emotionally distressed or your mind is very busy.

A CD was created to complement this meditation. Information on ordering the *Osho Nadabrahma* CD can be found on page 193.

If you choose not to order the CD, the meditation can certainly be done without it. I do not recommend using any other music for this technique.

STAGE ONE: *Humming (30 Minutes)*

Sit in a relaxed position with eyes closed and lips together. Start humming until you can feel the vibration throughout your body. (You'll probably be humming loudly enough to be heard by others.)

Just breathe comfortably; no special breathing techniques are needed. You can also alter the pitch or move your body smoothly and slowly if you feel like it. A point will come when the humming seems to continue by itself and you become the listener. Continue humming for thirty minutes.

STAGE TWO: *Circling with the Hands (15 minutes)*

(If you're not using the *Osho Nadabrahma* CD, set a timer for seven and a half minutes. I would recommend using a timer with a pleasing bell. You don't want to be jarred out of your meditative state.)

Now, still sitting and humming with eyes closed, place your palms up and, starting at the navel, move both hands forward and then divide them to make two large circles mirroring each other left and right. The idea is to move your hands in an outward circular motion. You bring the hands back toward the navel with the palms up and continue making slow circles horizontal to the floor. The movement should be so slow that at times there will appear to be no move- ment at all. Feel that you are giving energy to the universe.

After seven and a half minutes turn the hands palms down and start moving them in the opposite direction. Now the hands will come together toward the navel and then circle outward away from the sides of the body. Feel that you are taking energy in. As in the first stage, if you feel like moving any part of the rest of your body, do so slowly and mindfully.

STAGE THREE: *Rest (15 minutes)*

Now, just sit or lie absolutely still for fifteen minutes.

Take it easy for at least fifteen minutes after doing this technique. Get up slowly, being mindful not to rush into your next activity. You will feel a profound sense of well-being, of balance between your inner and outer worlds. Enjoy it. This powerful humming technique will open up a whole new world of healing, comfort, and creativity for you.

In addition to these two powerful practices for developing trust you can also try incorporating the following ideas into your everyday life.

Simple Reminders

1 ✦ Make a practice of listening to your intuition whenever you make a decision.

Should you go to that meditation class? Should you go to that party or a movie with a friend? What do you really feel like doing on your next day off? Pause for a moment; see if you can distinguish between the mind giving its opinion and your inner voice. At the beginning, your inner voice will be faint but the more you pay attention to it, and follow it, the more you will become accustomed to trusting it.

2 ✦ Try going outside in the early mornings and looking at the dawning light.

Listen to the early morning chatter of the birds; smell the freshness of the new day; feel the air, the cold, the warmth. Be present, mindful, paying attention to your self on this new day. Walk on the ground; feel it underneath your feet, supporting you. Try if for five minutes, longer if you like.

3 ✦ Before you go to bed at night, step outside for five minutes.

Look up at the stars, the moon, the night sky. Realize the vastness of our universe. Remember you are an intrinsic part of it. Look into the night; feel the darkness, the scent of evening. Listen to the silence, aware that the birds, the whole world is sleeping now. Walk on the ground. Feel it underneath your feet, supporting you. Then go inside, get into bed, and feel the comfort of the universe enveloping you as you fall asleep.

4 ✦ Listen to soothing lullabies as you go to sleep.

One CD I like is *Songs for the Inner Child* by Shaina Noll. Children are sung to and rocked to get them to fall asleep, to comfort them at night. There's nothing that says adults can't use comforting music to rock themselves to sleep as well. The reassuring effect of the lullabies will stay with you all night. The music will resonate with your heart and help you reconnect with the trust that lies within your heart.

7 ✦ The Peaceful Warrior:
The Art of Compassion

IF YOU WANT OTHERS TO BE HAPPY, PRACTICE COMPASSION. IF YOU
WANT TO BE HAPPY, PRACTICE COMPASSION.

—THE DALAI LAMA

A few years ago my friend David went to Hawaii for vacation
and left his teenage son alone at home for a few days. David
had reminded his son about not making a lot of noise but boys
will be boys, teenagers will be teenagers. Word got to David in
Hawaii that neighbors had complained one evening about
noise coming from his house when his son had some friends
over. They were apparently very angry. David's first reaction
was also anger. He was angry and resentful that he had to deal
with this situation when he was on vacation. He was angry
with his son and with the neighbors but also with himself,
thinking he "should" have done something to keep this situation from happening.

He decided to do the Gibberish meditation to discharge his
anger (see page 41). After a while he could feel himself dropping down into his center, beyond the level of the mind,
beyond the level of the hell that the mind was creating, and

found his haven of peace, calm, and stillness. As he rested in that place, he started to see the situation with more clarity. He remembered that his son had apologized for causing the trouble; he had said he'd forgotten about the neighbors and had sincerely tried to be quiet. In that space of quiet reflection, he remembered, too, that these neighbors had a tendency to overreact.

After a couple of days his perspective started to shift. He found himself relaxing about the whole thing. He felt ready to talk to his son in a calm way. He called his son and suggested that he apologize to the neighbor, which he willingly did. David's vacation was able to get back on track.

As David recounted the story, he noticed that he had started with himself, bringing compassion to himself because he thought his vacation was ruined. By calming himself down and realizing that it was not ruined, that it was just the mind creating a temporary disturbance, he was able to relax. He was able to enjoy the rest of his time in Hawaii. When he then talked with his son, he was able to be compassionate with him, accept his apology, and understand that he had not intentionally done anything to cause his father distress. He was simply being a teenager, totally involved in his own reality.

This is how meditation works. By bringing compassion to ourselves first we are able to release the angry turmoil the mind sometimes creates in the head, come to clarity, and reconnect with our happiness.

Compassion begins with oneself. And it is the highest form of love. The first step toward practicing compassion, toward taking the path of the "Peaceful Warrior," is to become aware of your own thoughts and actions. Observe yourself, with no judgment. Especially bring awareness to any self-critical or self-condemning habits you may have.

The second step is to bring in love for yourself whenever you remember. Think of all the positive things you have achieved and praise them—small things, like growing a good crop of tomatoes, cooking a tasty lasagna, rearranging your closet. As you make a habit of remembering to love yourself, in time, compassion will arise, toward yourself and toward others.

Perhaps you were brought up, as I was, believing that compassion means being nice to everybody, however badly they treat you. Meditation has taught me that allowing myself to be mistreated is not at all compassionate, not to myself and not to others. Nicey-nice "idiot compassion" helps no one.

Real compassion, I have discovered, knows how to say no, how to set boundaries, how to speak up for yourself, how to keep you safe from others' abuse. Practicing "fierce compassion" has taught me that by loving myself, I have more love to give to others. That is the way of the Peaceful Warrior.

The Peaceful Warrior addresses wrongs that are done to us in a compassionate way. The Peaceful Warrior understands that mistreatment is often unconscious and that by setting clear limits, we can often bring those who harm us to more awareness of their own actions while, at the same time, keeping them encompassed in our hearts. The Peaceful Warrior knows that self-love and compassionate clarity can go a long way toward transforming even the most difficult human relationships.

Not being able to love or receive love, not being able to share oneself causes great misery. Our soul needs love as much as the body needs food in order to survive. It is only through love that we know our soul, and that we are more than the body-mind. It is only through love that we can feel whole.

Fierce Compassion

Anyone can become angry—that is easy. But to be angry with
the right person, to the right degree, at the right time, for the
right purpose, and in the right way—that is not easy.

—ARISTOTLE

I was always taught not to be angry, not to raise my voice. To
be a "nice" girl, to be that kind of nicey-nice compassionate I
now know doesn't work. As a result, I never learned to defend
myself. People could get angry with me, attack me, dump their
anger on me, and I would just soak it all up. What built up in
me then was a lot of resentment and a lot of unexpressed
anger. Through my years of meditation and self-healing, I have
come to understand the difference between "idiot compassion" and "fierce compassion."

Compassion is not about having a bleeding heart full of
sympathy for others. Compassion is about having such a depth
of love that one is willing to do whatever it takes to bring
awareness to a situation. Don't get me wrong. I'm not saying
it's wrong to have sympathy for others. Sympathy is a wonderful quality. But the key is to bring conscious awareness to the
situation. Through a practice of meditation, we can, slowly,
slowly, understand ourselves; heal our pain; release our mental,
physical, and emotional tensions; and bring greater consciousness to events in our lives.

Anne's Story

Let me give you a little illustration of the contrast between
idiot and fierce compassion. My client Anne works for a large

insurance corporation in the sales and marketing department. She deals with people from all over the United States. Jennifer is a client in Wisconsin who Anne finds particularly difficult to deal with. She takes a long time to return phone calls and can be abrupt, sarcastic, and rude. Anne, on the other hand, is always courteous, timely with her work and strives to do a good job and to please.

As Anne became more aware of herself through her meditation practice and learned about compassion, she began to realize why she didn't enjoy working on the account managed by Jennifer. Phone conversations left her feeling frustrated and resentful that all the work was being done on her end. Her courtesy was met with rudeness and her hard work went unappreciated.

As Anne learned to have compassion for herself through meditation, she decided to talk with the director of human resource and asked to be taken off this particular account. To her relief she was told she didn't have to work on this account if she didn't want to. If only she had thought to ask earlier she could have saved herself a lot of grief.

A few months passed, then one day Jennifer came into town on business. By chance, Anne and Jennifer found themselves arriving early for a breakfast business meeting. They started to chat and Jennifer asked why Anne wasn't handling her account anymore. Anne took a deep breath and decided to tell Jennifer the truth. To her amazement Jennifer was not only willing to listen but admitted that she knew she could be a bit overbearing but had no idea she had such a devastating effect on people. She was grateful to Anne for having the courage to tell her the truth and acknowledged that she needed to make a few changes in her communication style.

She also became interested in meditation when Anne described her own work with it. Anne explained to Jennifer that she had found the Gibberish (see page 41) and Osho Dynamic (see page 44) techniques particularly useful in discharging her emotional stress. She had then been able to sit in silence and watch to gain deeper understanding, insight, and clarity about the situation.

Although they no longer work on the same account, they occasionally see each other and have developed a friendly relationship. By showing fierce compassion for herself, Anne was able to transform the situation. As the eighteenth-century French writer Voltaire said, "Cultivate your own garden."

DEVELOPING COMPASSION
FOR YOURSELF

However you are with yourself, you are with others. If you hate yourself you will hate others. Compassion, the way of the Peaceful Warrior, means loving yourself first.

Once upon a time there was a small forest. In that forest was a giant oak tree. But the oak tree was drooping its great branches. When asked what was wrong, the oak tree said, "I feel so defective because I am not as tall and majestic as the pine tree." The visitor looked at the pine tree and saw that it was becoming dry and brittle. When the visitor asked the pine tree what was wrong, the pine tree said, "I feel so inadequate because I can't creep like the grape vine." The visitor turned to the grape vine and noticed that it was wilting and all its leaves were falling off. When asked why, the grape vine responded that it felt imperfect because it was incapable of growing straight and tall on its own like the thistle.

The visitor turned to the thistle, which said, "I'm just being a thistle. I figure if the forest creator wanted an oak tree she would have planted an oak tree and if she wanted a pine tree she would have planted a pine tree. But she planted me instead so she must have wanted me."

We each have a unique purpose in life. We each have something to say, to share, and have our own way of saying it. It's a matter of self-acceptance, which is the same as being compassionate to ourselves and thankful for who we are.

In nature everything is the way it is. Roses bloom beautifully because they are not trying to be lavender or irises. A pear seed grows into a pear tree; a hazel seed grows into a hazel tree. Practice saying to yourself, as often as you'd like, "I am happy as I am." It starts with you: By allowing yourself to be who you are, by being compassionate with yourself, you will have an abundance of compassion to share. Love yourself, mother yourself, have mercy on yourself.

This is the way of the Peaceful Warrior.

The problem is, most of us were not taught to love ourselves. We were taught to *get* love from others or that we have to *do* something to become worthy of love, that we are not lovable just as we are. We learn a lot of "shoulds" and "oughts" that are impossible to fulfill. So the first step is to drop all "shoulds" and accept yourself the way you are.

MEDITATIONS FOR
CULTIVATING COMPASSION

 Here are a few techniques for awakening a sense of compassion, starting with compassion for yourself.

Picture Yourself as a Child

Picture yourself as a small child, as young as you can remember. If it is difficult to visualize yourself, gaze upon a picture of yourself at the youngest age possible. Send feelings of love and compassion to that small child. Maybe hug that child in your mind's eye.

If it is difficult to stay with love and compassion as other thoughts and feelings intrude, gently remind yourself to come back to thoughts and feelings of love and compassion. Be careful not to judge yourself if you find this exercise difficult. Be compassionate with yourself. Just do the best you can and recognize that it will become easier with time. (Can you see the irony of judging yourself harshly for not doing a compassionate exercise perfectly enough?)

Notice any self-hating thoughts that can creep in. Instead of increasing pain they can be used as stepping stones toward increased self-love by saying, "I've been so hard on myself, for so long, that I can scarcely do this exercise at all. I need as much love and compassion as I can allow myself."

Next, picture yourself as an older child and do the same thing. Don't forget to hug yourself at least in your mind. Move up to puberty (an age where we all especially need compassion and hugs). Continue this process in steps of five or ten years until you reach your present age. Now do the same thing you've been doing for your younger selves—bathe yourself in love and compassion while hugging yourself.

If you experience any difficulty doing this exercise, try to just observe it. Allow it to be there; accept it without judgment. Insights and understandings about yourself will arise.

Cherish Yourself, Cherish Others

Begin by spending five minutes at the beginning of the day remembering that we all want the same things (to be happy and be loved) and that we are all connected to one another. Love and happiness are what everyone wants even though sometimes we are not able to admit it to ourselves; perhaps because we believe we don't deserve it or we're afraid we'll never have it. The first step to getting something we want is to admit that we want it. By cherishing ourselves, then others, we can start to tend the seeds of love in our hearts so that they can grow and bloom into a full flowering of love and happiness.

Now, take five minutes to breathe in—cherishing yourself—and breathe out—cherishing others. If you think about people you have difficulty cherishing, extend your cherishing to them anyway. Throughout the day, extend this attitude to everyone you meet. Practice cherishing everyone from the clerk in the supermarket to your least favorite client to your partner or parent or children; cherish the people you love (including yourself) and the people you dislike. Allow yourself to feel the boundless love and appreciation that already exist in your heart.

Karuna

In Tibetan Buddhism a great emphasis is given to developing compassion. Compassion (karuna) is said to be the "trembling of the open heart in response to suffering." A practice often used goes like this:

While sitting silently you hold a sense of connection to yourself or to another and repeat one phrase over and over, such as "May you be safe, may you be happy, may you be healthy, may you live with ease." You can use these or similar phrases as long as they are positive in orientation, emphasizing what is beautiful in life.

In compassion practice the idea is to tune in to the suffering aspect of the person's life. It is the awareness of suffering that gives rise to compassion.

Generally you use just one phrase, which you repeat over and over. The traditional phrase is "May you be free from suffering." Another way might be, "May you be free from your pain and sorrow." If the person has a particular form of suffering, the phrase can

reflect this, such as, "May you be free from your grief," or fear, or ill-
ness or whatever.

Some people find that this phrase "may you be free from"
can lead to a subtle sense of aversion, as though we were saying
"may you be rid of." This is not necessarily what is meant in the traditional phrase but some people may take it this way. In that case
you might want to say "I care about your suffering" or "I care about
your pain and sorrow."

Compassion practice is an invaluable ally in the journey of
awakening. It's like finding gold on the path and can be practiced at
any point in your meditation journey. It reminds us over and over
that suffering is an inevitable aspect of life and thereby connects us
with all living beings.

The tremendous value of compassion can often be, paradoxi-
cally, when we are most overwhelmed by suffering, whether our
own, or another's.

In an incredible way the compassion practice connects us
directly with the truth of our present experience. "May I be free
from suffering," or "I care about this suffering." Very soon the heart
starts to soften in relation to the painful state of mind. The state
seems less threatening, less alien, less overwhelming. What starts to
pervade the mind, in coexistence with the difficult emotion, is the
flavor of compassion, which the phrase has started to evoke. With
the combination of these two parts, there is a profound acceptance
of the situation just as it is, an acceptance of oneself just as one is,
and an acceptance of the human condition just as we are.

Our meditation practice unfolds most gracefully when we
can experience a mind state just as it is without *any* wish for the
experience to be different.

Compassion can become an avenue for the transformation
of the difficult experience through a deep acceptance. The compassionate heart can grow big enough to hold the pain without com-
plaining.

Not only is that heart uncomplaining, it is actually filled with sweetness because compassion is not a state of suffering but a divine abiding. Because compassion is ignited by contact with suffering, it is not an exuberant or purely delightful state. It can be said to be like the feeling at sunset—beauty tinged with a little bit of sadness at the passing of the day. If the sadness becomes too strong then it can tip over into pity or grief. But when the factor of equanimity is also present, then compassion can hold the suffering in a balanced way. Cradled in the arms of compassion, our hearts can relax into healing themselves and opening up as wide as the world.

Simple Reminders

Here are a few ideas for helping you cultivate compassion for yourself:

1 ✦ Do one thing to show compassion for yourself every day.

Make a commitment to this practice for two weeks. Then see if you can do one thing a day that is compassionate for another person.

2 ✦ Have a date with yourself.

Take yourself to your favorite art gallery, to the beach, to a play or a movie. Have lunch at your favorite restaurant. Do something that is especially for you; no one else has to be considered.

3 ✦ Bring flowers to work to brighten your day.

If anyone asks, just say they came from someone who cares about you.

4 ✦ Appreciate yourself.

Stop and take a few deep breaths. For a few moments feel appreciation for yourself. Give yourself appreciation for no reason. Appreciate yourself for the sheer enjoyment of it. Now think of one thing you really appreciate about someone you know. Let her know in some way that you appreciate her.

5 ✦ Bring awareness to your relationships with friends, family, coworkers.

Experiencing friendship, affinity, and belonging are helpful in developing compassion. Take five minutes and just sit and feel the connection with one or several of these people. Feel your heart opening to yourself and to them. Get in touch with the *experience* of having that person or those people in your life.

8 ✦ Lunchtime Enlightenment: Integrating Work and Meditation

People often tell me that they don't have time to meditate. Sometimes I answer by asking, "You have time for lunch, don't you?" Meditation is no more time-consuming than a lunch break. In fact, meditation can be your lunch break, as I explained recently to a group of staffers at the *San Francisco Chronicle,* San Francisco's morning newspaper.

Phyllis Kittleson, from the *Chronicle's* Human Resources Department, which organized the event, had arranged for everyone attending to have a sack lunch waiting for them. Our session was limited to forty-five minutes, as newspaper people are always working under pressure of a deadline. Once everyone was seated, I invited them to unwrap their food and eat slowly, enjoying each aroma, taste, and texture. I suggested that they try as much as possible to eat with their eyes closed. Though they were surprised by this unusual request, they quickly agreed to try.

While people ate, I brought their attention to their bodies

sitting comfortably on the chairs. I suggested that they be aware as well of the flavor of the food in their mouths, how much they were enjoying the lunch they had chosen, how easily their digestive system was processing the food. I encouraged them to be totally present, to engage for this short period in only what they were doing—eating lunch and nothing else. Normally, I had been told, most people who work at the *Chronicle* eat lunch at their desks and continue working at the same time. Traffic from the street, ringing telephones, laughter, and conversations punctuate most of their lunch breaks. As sounds intruded into our lunch break—the sound of the door opening and closing, the rustling of lunch bags as people came in late, even the sound of my voice—I incorporated these interruptions into the meditation. I wanted people to learn to stay relaxed and focused without being disturbed by other people's activity.

This is one of the special tricks of meditation. I find that once people have experienced this feeling of relaxed focus, once they understand that it is possible for the body to remain calm and centered though they are surrounded by busyness, they find it much easier to stay relaxed under similar conditions in their offices.

At the end of the session, everyone said they had enjoyed eating lunch this way. They reported being more satisfied, less anxious about how much they ate, more at ease with the whole process of eating. We laughed as one woman said it was fine eating with her eyes closed until the tomatoes started dripping out of her sandwich. Another woman commented that she felt as if she were falling asleep. I told her that this was a sign that she had reached a place of deep relaxation that can be very refreshing and revitalizing for the body. A man commented that he couldn't believe how quickly the time had gone by.

How do you usually eat lunch? Can you take some time just for yourself? Maybe five minutes? Maybe longer? Nobody needs to know that you're meditating while munching on your sandwich or salad. Nobody needs to know that you have chosen lunchtime as the doorway into the private haven inside yourself: a place where everything is accepted; a place where you do only what you are doing; a place where you can pour all of your energy into yourself, recharge your batteries, and from which you return to work feeling relaxed, calm, and positive.

LUNCHTIME MEDITATIONS

 Here are some suggestions for lunchtime meditations you might try.

Eating with Awareness

Close your office door or find another place where you can eat your lunch without being disturbed. Eat slowly and deliberately, enjoying each flavor and sensation that arises, the crisp and juicy sweetness of an apple, the salty crunch of a chip, the fragrant comfort of a steaming cup of tea. Chew slowly and feel your body receiving the food. Eat what your stomach wants and only as much as it wants, not what your eyes want. Let your stomach decide what you drink. Drink slowly, enjoying the taste, temperature, and aroma of your favorite beverage. Breathe. Be with yourself.

This is a shorter variation of the eating meditation that I recommend when you are pressed for time. You might also find it useful when traveling or "on the road," for example on airplanes, car trips, picnics, or at airports, bus depots, or a busy restaurant.

Walk in the Park

Go for a walk in a park or other place where there are trees and flowers, if possible. Walk slowly. Let the body relax. Breathe. Let your eyes enjoy the colors of the flowers, the trees, the sky. Let your ears enjoy the sounds of nature or of soothing music if you are wearing headphones. Bring your awareness to your feet. Let them enjoy feeling the ground as you walk. Be aware of the differences between various surfaces, the resilience of a grassy lawn, the crunch of gravel, the uneven paving stones of a garden path. Sit for a while on a bench or on the ground with your back against a tree. Let the tension sink out of your body and into the ground. Spend a long moment looking at a tree or up into the clear blue sky.

Just Sit There

Sit in a comfortable position on a chair or on the floor for five minutes, longer if you can. Make sure that your clothing is not constricted so the body can relax. Sit with the back relatively straight. Close your eyes. Wearing a blindfold can help take the stress off the eyes. Relax the body. Let your awareness move inside and begin to observe your breathing. There is no right way to breathe, so there is no need to change your breathing. Only watch.

This simple technique can reduce the secretion of the adrenal glands and lower blood pressure. Generally after only five to ten minutes, the secretion of adrenaline is less, and you feel this difference. Fatigue is relieved, and the body's store of energy is renewed.

Listen to Music

Choose some soothing music and sit or lie down and listen to it, with or without headphones, depending on your situation. *Shamanic Dream* by Anugama, with its gentle earth rhythm, and *The Mystik*

Dance by El Hadra, with a rhythm that corresponds to the breath and heartbeat, are two of my favorites. You will find other suggestions for appropriate music at the back of the book. You might like to try my *Guided Relaxation* CD (see page 194). Close your eyes and feel as if the sounds of the music are circling toward you. You are the center. Try not to judge or analyze the music in any way. Just feel the sound all around you, falling on you from every side. Relax your senses and let the sounds enter you, making you more liquid and open. Sounds are not heard in the ears. The head is for words, not for sounds. The center for sounds is deep down in the belly. Allow the sounds of the music to take you deep into your own center, which is in the belly, two inches below the navel. At your center, all is silence, peace, and calm. With practice, this meditation will help you stay connected with your center, your inner haven of silence and stillness, no matter what sounds are around you.

Go Horizontal

Simply lie down, on a couch, on the floor, in a park, wherever you can that's appropriate for you. Close your eyes. Allow the body to let go. Allow the tension to drain downward into the ground, or into the couch or floor. Feel the support underneath you. Rest. Let go. This meditation is particularly good for people who feel they have "no support," who feel they have to do everything themselves.

Bring your awareness to every part of your body. Begin at the center, two inches below the navel. Then move your awareness down the right leg, back up the left leg and all the way up your left side to your head. Then come back down the right side, returning to your center. Breathe. Feel the feelings.

Whatever amount of time you have, no matter where you are at your lunch break, whether you're in a cubicle or out in a park, you can turn this time into meditation time. It's not a question of time but of understanding what meditation is, and what it is not.

As you practice the ideas in this chapter, you may come up with your own ideas for practice. It is surprising how incorporating a few simple techniques can not only transform your lunchtime but your whole day as well.

Bringing It Home

The ordinary arts we practice everyday at home are of more importance to the soul than their simplicity might suggest.

—THOMAS MOORE

Work is not just what we do in our office or on our lunch hour. Many of us dread the chores at home—cooking, cleaning, doing the laundry, paying the bills—at least as much. Here again, by bringing a relaxed awareness to these tasks we can not only get more quality time with ourselves, but our homes will also more likely reflect the sense of ease.

There is a story of the enlightened Japanese Zen master Bankei. He was an ordinary man. One day he was working in his garden. A man came to visit him, a seeker, a man in search of a master. He asked Bankei, "Gardener, where is the master?" Bankei laughed and said, "Wait a moment. Go to that yonder door, open it and go in. Inside you will find the master."

So the man went around and came inside. He saw Bankei sitting on a throne, the same man who was the gardener outside. The seeker said: "Are you kidding me? Get down from this throne. This is sacrilegious, you don't pay any respect to the master."

Bankei got down, sat on the ground, and replied: "Now then it is difficult. Now you will not find the master here because I am the master."

You see, the ego likes us to do grandiose things, things that make us (the mind) feel important. Tasks like weeding the garden, cleaning the dishes, taking out the trash all seem so mediocre, so "beneath" us. Yet by bringing a certain quality of consciousness to any activity we can transform it into an activity *worthy* of our time. Whether we are taking a shower or hanging out with our kids, washing the car, cooking, paying bills, doing laundry, or jogging—we can bring the quality of present-moment consciousness to it and thus begin to dissolve the boundaries between chores and play. Just remember the three essential elements: relaxation, nonjudgment, and awareness, and any activity can become a meditation.

This notion has deep roots. Eighteenth-century Hasidism, for example, rejected asceticism in favor of doing everything with joy and awareness and thus suffusing even the most mundane task with a sense of spirituality. Rather than renouncing, Hasidism values celebrating the ordinary. Similarly, in the Zen tradition the ordinary activity of flower arrangement is used as a method to reach to meditation, and in the Sufi tradition, rug weaving is used. In the Christian tradition the Benedictine monks see their prayer, love, and devotion in simple ordinary tasks: chopping wood, cooking, cleaning, fetching water from the well.

I remember how I used to feel about cleaning. I thought of it as something arduous that took me away from what I really wanted to do; it was a waste of my time. Slowly, through my practice of meditation, I realized that I was suffering from a judgment my mind was making and I decided to try an experiment.

I would look at cleaning from a different perspective, as an exercise in witnessing, to see the workings of my ego in an everyday activity such as this. What I discovered is that I was bringing a "that'll do" attitude to cleaning. I was not a perfectionist ("there's still a bit of fluff on the floor,") nor a reluctant cleaner ("it doesn't need doing, it's not even dirty"). No, I was a quick "lick and polish" type.

When I looked a little deeper, I noticed that I brought this same attitude to many other activities, like cleaning my car, doing laundry, shopping for groceries. I tried to pass through these sorts of "chores" at the speed of light, not really present, and even a bit resentful that I had to be doing them at all. I certainly never *enjoyed* myself doing them. Enjoyment was reserved for those activites my ego decided were more worthwhile: chitchatting with friends, going to parties, watching movies. And yet when I looked at those things more deeply, I realized I wasn't always enjoying myself doing *them,* either. My mind told me I should be, but sometimes I clearly wasn't. I was letting my ego decide things, instead of my heart.

Everything changed when I decided to put my heart into cleaning. When I started cleaning *for myself,* so that my house would be more beautiful to live in, the act of cleaning took on a totally different feeling. I even noticed that I overcame my aversion to dirt, realizing that dirt itself is perfectly innocent and is easily removed with just a touch of awareness and a love of clarity (and occasionally a bit of elbow grease).

I can see now, by bringing a conscious awareness to it, that cleaning is not about shiny bathroom taps or fulfilling somebody's expectations. It's about the expression and experience of my creativity, my beauty, my dignity, my joy, my love. And about my unawareness and resistance to being clear with myself.

When I clean now, I listen to my favorite music, put on a kettle to make myself a fresh pot of tea, and throw open all the windows to catch a breeze. Then afterward I carve out a precious interlude of time for myself. If it's warm I sit on the porch and bask in the sunshine, with the birds, the trees, my cat, the blossoms. I try to just rest in the present moment, not be anywhere but here and *enjoy what I have.*

We are all given a choice each day. We can react negatively to the demands made on us or we can choose to transform the negative into the meaningful. Attitude is all. If I do not endow my work with meaning, no one else will. If I don't recognize the value of what I am doing no one else will.

It's not difficult to see where our aversion to cleaning comes from. Perhaps as kids we were constantly being drilled about living a "clean" life. Maybe we were always being told to straighten up our rooms or take the trash out or keep the living room tidy. However we were treated around cleaning as kids will rear its ugly head again in our adult attitudes and get in the way of a clear perspective on ourselves and keeping our house clean *now.*

Your "chore" may not be cleaning. It may be grocery shopping or cooking or making the bed. You can bring this same quality of presence and awareness to any of these activities. Try it. You'll see. Relax, don't judge; just watch and these activities you once dreaded can become your meditations.

As Gunilla Norris tells us in her book *Being Home,* "When we clean and order our homes, we are somehow cleaning and ordering ourselves."

Our household tasks must get done, so we have two choices: We can either do them resentfully or we can find a way to enjoy doing them. See if there is some way you can make your chores more fun.

Try this process of self-inquiry: Ask yourself what it is that you hate about a particular household task, whether it's doing dishes, taking out the trash, doing laundry, whatever. You may want to reread Chapter 4 on nonjudgment. See if you can gain some insight into any old ideas that were put in your head during childhood. This understanding will help to free you from their grip over your present reality.

Ask yourself these questions:

+ Were you ashamed to bring friends home to your house? Because it was dirty? Untidy? Too immaculate? Too perfect?
+ What were the special treats of your childhood? Did you have to tidy your room or do your chores in order to earn them?
+ Did your parents fight over who was doing what in the home?
+ What did you learn from your parents about housework that made you feel good? That made you feel bad?

MEDITATIONS FOR THE WORK AT HOME

Working in Silence

Try this: Do your task in silence, being present, right there with what you are doing. If it's doing the dishes that's a problem for you, for example, make it a meditation. Make a conscious effort to be fully present, rather than having your mind be elsewhere. Clean the dishes slowly and mindfully, without trying to get through them in a hurry, but rather with your full presence. Surrender yourself to the present moment. Being total with an activity can help transform your consciousness around that activity.

Preparing Food

Bring your full awareness to what you are doing. If possible don't talk. Move slowly around the kitchen. Whether you are chopping vegetables, preparing a sauce, or mixing pancake batter, bring a quality of awareness to the food and to the people you are preparing the food for, including, and especially, yourself. Savor the smells, the textures, aromas, and tastes of the different ingredients. Become aware of your body. Relax it. Feel your feet on the ground. As the food will probably be going in your body, listen to it. Is it happy about what you are preparing? Again, this shift in attention can transform how you feel about doing this task.

Planting Your Garden

Plants live in the earth and have a relaxing, grounding effect upon us. Maybe you are fortunate enough to have a garden. If not, try this with your houseplants. When you take care of your plants and garden, do it slowly, mindfully. As you weed and water your plants remember yourself. Remember you are a part of this whole universe as are the plants and the earth. Receive the energy of the plants as you give energy to them. Enjoy their presence in your life. Participate with them in a delightful appreciation of life.

There is a divine order happening as a backdrop to our daily routines. Order uplifts us—it is important for our spirit: night into day; sunrise, sunset; the order of the changing seasons. We are perhaps unaware of it as the humdrum of life beckons our attention. By focusing on order we can bring the sacred into the mundane. By tidying, cleaning, gardening, cooking, making the bringing of order into a meditation we can transform all our "chores" into acts of self-love and self-care.

9 ✦ The Alchemy of Love:
Going Deeper

FOR ONE HUMAN BEING TO LOVE ANOTHER: THAT IS PERHAPS THE
MOST DIFFICULT TASK OF ALL. . . . THE WORK FOR WHICH ALL OTHER
WORK IS BUT PREPARATION. IT IS A HIGH INDUCEMENT TO THE INDI-
VIDUAL TO RIPEN . . . A GREAT EXACTING CLAIM UPON US. SOME-
THING THAT CHOOSES US OUT AND CALLS US TO VAST THINGS.

—RAINER MARIA RILKE

In my younger days and early on in my meditation journey, I
fell in love with a married man who worked in the office
where I was doing a summer job. Consciously and unconsciously I had always been seeking love—looking for ful-
fillment through friends, coworkers, or a love relationship. But
this was the first time that the love was not reciprocated. I
didn't like the reality I was faced with, and this caused an argument within me. What was I going to do with the love I felt
for him? Shut it down and hate him? Hate myself? Guess what
I got from my argument with reality? Pain and suffering—
because I was shutting my love down.

One day over that same summer I was sitting with my meditation teacher in a counseling session and he noticed that I

seemed to be suffering some emotional distress. I realized it must be about the married man. I told him that I had fallen in love with a man but that there was no point because he was married. I should not love someone who was married.

John, my meditation teacher, said, "What is the truth? Do you love this man?"

"Yes," I replied. And with that yes, I felt such relief and deep relaxation at saying the truth of my heart. It felt so good to say it. I realized I had been judging and condemning myself and creating a lot of internal tension because I believed it was wrong to love a man who was married. I was in denial of my own heart. I was in a fight with myself. My heart loved and my mind said I should not love. I was divided. This was what was causing my stress.

"Does he know that you love him?" asked John. "No," I replied. "Well, you must tell him," John continued. "Whenever you love someone you must tell them, and then you will be free of it. And you must say it to him, not in a letter but out loud. You have always been strategic with your love, Pragito: I'll love you if you'll love me. It's time to learn about unconditional love. True love doesn't use strategy. It just states its case, unattached to the outcome. It is not a bargain, but a gift, a giving."

I knew he was right although my ego and my pride were burning at the thought of telling someone I loved him who didn't return those same feelings. But I decided to do it anyway. As I told this man of my love for him I noticed that all my fear disappeared and I felt my heart, my self-confidence, my self-respect, and my self-love become much stronger. It was a very powerful lesson about love. When love is allowed to flow, fear will always disappear. Love is not about taking what you can get from another but about what can you give. It's about allowing what is in your own heart and giving it to another person. Whether they love you in return or not is not the important part.

As soon as I came out of denial, owned the truth of my heart, and told this man of my love, I was free. I was no longer divided. I was at one with myself. As it happened, this man received my love very gracefully, which was beautiful for me and another layer of the lesson. If he had not received what I was giving him, it would have been very painful. What we want the most when we give someone a gift, is that they will receive it. So we need to thank them for receiving our gift. If people do not want the love we have to give them, then it is not wise to go on trying to give it to them. We are simply creating pain for ourselves.

When I told this man of my love for him my heart opened and I was able to move on and meet someone who was available. My relating changed after that time. Instead of looking for love, I started to give love and found that it came back to me in a greater abundance than I ever could have imagined. I found that the source of love is within me, not out there with somebody else. What I was seeking, I already had.

With this new awareness, meditation then helped me to continue the exploration of my own heart so that I could become a cause of love, rather than being at the mercy of someone else for my happiness. I chose techniques that would loosen feelings and expand my ability to relate to others, to care, and to love. The specific meditations that helped open my heart were the Mystic Rose meditation, and the Moving meditations in Chapter 1. They helped me to heal the pain in my heart and erase old fear patterns that kept my heart contracted.

I found the joy in mutual giving, which replaced the friction of reciprocating demands. I learned to have compassion for myself and to grow in my ability to accept and give love. I felt, as the Zen poet Ryokan says:

The rain has stopped, the clouds have drifted away, and the
weather is clear again. If your heart is pure, then all things in
your world are pure. Then the moon and the flowers will
guide you along the way.

I tell this story to illustrate how a pivotal situation in my life
rerouted me on my search for love. From out to in, from "the
other" to myself. Meditation was the garden in which I could
plant this fragile seed, to nurture it, tend it, cultivate it so that it
could flower. I learned, too, that the real opposite to love is not
hate but fear, that in fear I was shrinking and in love I
expanded. In fear I was closed and in love my heart opened.
And a tremendous trust arose from my heart, a trust in myself
and my ability to love.

Speaking the truth of our hearts brings us freedom from the
beliefs of the mind, freedom to love life, to love ourselves, to
love others. Life loves us, if we will allow it to. My situation
helped me understand this. It was not a punishment, as I had
first thought; I was not being foolish, I was simply being
human. A human loving another human. It was the condi-
tioned beliefs in my head that were the problem, not the love
in my heart.

So many of us are tremendously afraid of love. How do we
move through this fear? Meditation helps us focus on being
more loving, on our inner journey. By and by the fear-creating
manipulations of the mind will recede. With vigilant awareness, we can allow the love in our hearts to arise and not be
destroyed by unconscious fears.

We can learn a lot simply by seeing how we avoid love. Do
we cut ourselves off, telling ourselves we don't need it? Are we
too needy, desperate, and clinging? Do we smother people,
which makes them run away? Meditation can bring us into
balance by focusing on loving ourselves first. Once we love

ourselves, the love tends to radiate; we become open and soft and beauty shines from our beings. Only when we love ourselves can love happen to us. Love, like meditation, cannot be bought or bartered for. It has to be earned. Then it happens to us, a gift from existence. Whenever love happens, receive it, accept it, enjoy it. It will bring you an interdependence, neither dependent nor independent: balanced, in the middle.

> Meditate, find out your own center first. Before you can relate with somebody else, relate with yourself: that is the basic requirement to be fulfilled. Without it nothing is possible. With it, nothing is impossible.

> —OSHO

Over the years I have found that by remembering to bring a loving attitude to myself and to daily interactions, more love is generated both in myself and in the world. Here are a few reminders to carry love into the world:

Simple Reminders to Awaken Loving Feelings

- ✦ Become more loving toward yourself.
- ✦ Be more loving toward people. Love the trees, flowers, neighbors, friends, coworkers. Consciously look for ways that you can be more loving. To give, without any thought of any bargain, of any return.
- ✦ As the bumper sticker says, "Practice random acts of kindness." It will make *you* feel good.
- ✦ Start small. Smile more at people on the street, at the girl at the checkout counter, at your colleagues at work.

+ Be helpful to people, and whenever you have a choice of being generous or doing things "by the book," be generous. Give that waitress an extra dollar tip; call a friend who is having difficulties.

+ Tell your loved ones that you love them. Whenever you love someone, tell them. Even if you think they know, remind them from time to time. We all need to hear that we are loved.

MEDITATIONS FOR OPENING TO LOVE

The following techniques are particularly beneficial for bringing more love into your life. You might also like to try my CD *Opening to Love Meditation* (information for ordering is on page 194).

Sixty-Second Stop

This first technique is something you can just carry with you and use whenever you're feeling disconnected from your heart. Close your eyes. Become aware of your heart. You might want to place your hand on your heart. Bring in a memory of a person, place, or event that brings you a lot of joy. Feel the happiness filling your heart with that memory. This powerful yet simple technique will encourage the love in your heart to grow and will attract more love to you.

Feeling More Loving

The heart is not only a physical mechanism; it is also a spiritual vehicle. The more aware you become of your heart, the more love you will feel, because the love is already inside you. It just has to be awakened. When you hold the hand of a friend, or hug a friend, do it with awareness. See whether you are releasing warmth or not. See whether your warm vital life energy is flowing into them or not. Bring your attention there. Energy will follow where you bring your attention. Try this for one day, for one hour, or for just one meeting. Experiment in different situations with different people.

When you look at somebody, look with eyes of love, because otherwise the physical eyes are just stones, hard and cold with no welcome in them. When you look at people, pour love through the eyes. When you walk around, radiate love all around. If you have to imagine it at the beginning, that is okay. After a very short time it will become a reality. People will start feeling that you have a warmer personality, that coming close to you feels tremendously good—a well-being arises. Make this a conscious effort—to become more aware of love and to release more love.

Couples Meditation #1

Here's a simple yet powerful technique for creating a feeling of deep harmony between partners in a couple. It's a humming meditation and the sound and vibration of the humming helps bring both partners to the same frequency. I recommend that you get hold of the CD *Osho Nadabrahma,* which was created for this meditation. (You'll find information on how to obtain this CD on page 193.)

When I work with couples in counseling sessions I always suggest that they find some time, at least once a week, to meditate together. It can help if there have been any disagreements or upsets or if you have a difficult topic to discuss, for example financial disagreements, or problems with your kids or in-laws. If you can get in the habit of meditating together before discussing your difficult topics, both of you will tend to be more relaxed and centered for the discussion, which can smooth the way to a more creative outcome.

You also might want to do this technique simply as a way to be together nonverbally, to enjoy each other, taking some time out from daily activities. It's a great way to move from "doing together" to "being together." I can almost guarantee that this Couples meditation will have a very positive effect on your relationship.

You'll want to set aside at least an hour for this meditation. Dim lighting is best. You can do this with or without clothes on.

Find a place where you're both comfortable and just sit silently together, facing each other, for fifteen minutes, holding each other's hands crosswise. This will help to harmonize and balance the energies between you.

Breathe together for a few minutes. Exhale together, inhale together. Get in tune with each other. Breathe as if you are one organism, not two bodies but one. Look into each other's eyes very softly. Take time to enjoy each other, to be present with each other.

Then close your eyes and hum together for thirty minutes. If you don't have the CD then use a timer to know when the thirty minutes have passed. Either with the CD or without is good but I don't recommend any other music. Thirty minutes might seem like a long time but sometimes it can take us at least fifteen minutes to start to move downward from the chattering mind toward our center down in the belly. The results will be most beneficial if you can do the full thirty minutes, but if you find that that's just too tough, try for at least fifteen and build up from there.

Start humming loudly with your mouths open. This will create a vibration throughout your whole body. No special breathing is necessary, and you can alter the pitch or move your body slowly if you want to.

After a short while you will feel your energies meeting, merging, and uniting.

At the end, slowly open your eyes. Try to spend another five minutes in silence together enjoying each other's presence.

Couples Meditation #2

I teach another variation on the Couples meditation that is based on Tantric techniques. Even though the word "Tantra" is by now familiar to many people, there has been also a lot of misconception around its meaning. The ancient art of Tantra that originated in the East teaches an acceptance of who we are as a whole, from the dense dimension of our physical form to the more subtle layers of the spirit.

In most religious and spiritual teachings, we have been taught to create a division between body, mind, and spirit, and to undermine the physical form as something "nonspiritual" or "lower." In Tantra, the body is not seen as something to be ashamed of but rather as a sacred doorway to our innermost self. It is seen as a sacred temple where the soul resides and is given the full respect and attention that such a temple deserves. Tantra is an invitation to make each and every aspect of the human experience an opportunity to rejoice and be present in awareness. Through this, all opposites will be reunited in a harmonious and healing unity. For example, Tantra includes in its teaching using sexual energy as a doorway to meditation and higher states of consciousness.

For this next exercise I recommend listening to the music *Tantric Heart: Music for Lovers* by Shastro (you'll find more information about this CD on page 194). If you can't get hold of this CD, you can certainly try the technique without music or with other suitable music.

Try to find a time to be with your partner when you are awake and fresh, not just late at night after a long day of work. I suggest that you set aside fifteen to twenty minutes for this exercise. Lie down naked, facing your partner, close enough for your bellies to touch. Allow your breath to drop deep into the belly and bring your inhale and exhale into the same rhythm. Try to maintain your focus on the breathing and slowly feel the merging that happens as the two breaths become one and the boundary of the two bodies begins to soften. Feel the relaxation between you two deepen as you rest into the atmosphere invoked by the music. (If the energy between you is inspired to move in a more sensual way, let it happen, remaining in touch with the sacred quality of oneness that you have just established.)

At the end of the exercise take a few moments to be together with eyes closed and feel your connection and love for yourself, and at the same time, your connection and love for your partner. See if you can get a sense of feeling alone yet not alone. This is one of the gifts of meditation, to gain a sense of ourselves and at the same time our connectedness with others. You might think of two trees standing next to each other, rooted in themselves but the branches touching.

These techniques are perfect nonverbal ways to be together and can bring you into a wonderful harmony with each other that can not only deepen your union but also help dissolve any difficulties you might have been experiencing together. They can bring you in touch with the essence of the love and respect you share with each other. Couples meditation can give you a solid foundation for going deeper. Rather than just relating from the more superficial layers of mind and personality, you can begin to resonate in greater harmony with each other.

If you've been experiencing some strain in your relationship or there's just been "no time" for sensuality, it may take some time, even a few sessions, to become comfortable in your bodies together again. If you and your partner have been out of touch with each other physically, I would recommend committing one evening or morning a week to the practice of these techniques. I'd be very surprised if you don't experience a reblooming of intimacy between you.

The Mystic Rose Meditation

The Mystic Rose meditation is longer, more powerful, and will take you into a deeper place inside yourself than any of the shorter techniques. It requires a greater committment, not just of your time but of your willingness to dig deep within yourself. The benefits are also much longer lasting and, as they are more deeply rooted within you, will bring a profound transformation on the emotional, physical, and mental levels.

This technique was created by Osho as the second in a series of what he called "Meditative Therapies." Because many of us have lost the capacity to sit in silence, these techniques were developed to work as a bridge, to clear the ground for deeper meditation. They are perfect for handling the pressures of our twenty-first-century lifestyle, designed as they were to release us from years of repressed emotions, physical tensions in the body, and old mental ideas and beliefs that no longer work for us. So much energy is tied up in unexpressed emotion. By letting the feelings out, we can then go into deeper and deeper layers, releasing and healing.

They open up our whole energy system, working on the emotional body, doing emotional clearing, releasing stress, pain, anguish, despair. The physical and psychological transformation that can happen through the practice of these techniques creates the potential for more love, more gracefulness, more flexibility, and more joyousness in all aspects of our lives.

I chose the Mystic Rose for this book because it is one of the most powerful and simple forms of meditation ever devised. I consider it the greatest revolution in meditation since Vipassana was developed by the Buddha 2,500 years ago. It is a three-week process of three hours each day. The first week is for laughter, for expressing our natural joy and love of life. The laughter week is a great way to open up more to our feelings. The second week is for crying, for a deep healing and unburdening of the heart. After releasing pent-up emotions through crying, we are ready to simply sit and observe, which is the core of meditation. The third week, which Osho called the "Watcher on the Hills," is for sitting silently in deep meditation. It brings about an integration, a closure.

The Mystic Rose is a great technique both for people new to meditation and for experienced meditators.

I recommend drinking a lot of water while doing this technique. When we release tensions from the body, it is a good idea to keep the body well hydrated. I also recommend doing this meditation in a group, and with a trained instructor, if at all possible. If after trying it out yourself or with a few friends (see page 194 for information on my *Mystic Rose* CD), you find that you'd like to work with an instructor, you can find information on where this meditation is held on my Web site, www.pragito.com or at www.osho.com. You will also find information about training as an instructor.

If three hours a day seems a bit daunting, start with something much simpler, like five minutes a day. Then build up to ten or fifteen minutes each day. The important things are that you devote the same amount of time to each stage and that you do the stages in sequence: laughing, crying, watching. Remember, however, that the most powerful benefit will come when you can do three hours each day for three weeks.

STAGE ONE: *Laughter*

Begin by shouting "Yaa-hoo!" a few times. Try shouting it with your arms raised over your head. This promotes a feeling of well-being and positivity in the body. Many people find they start laughing just from saying "Ya-hoo!"

Now, sitting or lying down, eyes open or closed, laugh for no reason at all. For three hours. If it helps to tell yourself some jokes, or to listen to some taped laughter, that would be a great way to get started. (You can order my tape of laughter from my Web site, www.pragito.com.)

You may prefer to lie on your back. Some people find that this helps relax their stomach muscles and allows energy to move more easily. Some people cover themselves with a sheet, or hold their legs in the air, to help bring out the laughing, giggling child in them. Whatever you need to do to find your inner laughter is fine. If you're doing this with others, some eye contact is also fine.

After three hours of laughing, sit silently, watching for fifteen minutes. You don't have to become serious, you just want to center your energy before the end of the session.

It's an extraordinary experience to laugh for three hours for no reason. I remember the first time I did the Mystic Rose. I was so worried that I wouldn't be able to laugh, especially not for so long. The wonderful thing about laughter is that it brings us to the present moment and when we are in the present moment, worry does not exist. We only worry when the mind takes us to the future or the past. So if you're worried about laughing for three hours, just jump in and start laughing and watch as the waves of laughter chase your worry away.

You've probably never just laughed freely like this, so don't be surprised if you come up against some blocks. If you do, try shouting "Yaa-hoo!" or do gibberish (nonsense sounds) until laughter arises again. We are all born full of laughter. But our laughter has been repressed by teachers, parents, society. Now, in this laughter week you will simply release and reclaim all that dammed-up energy.

Here are a few tips to help you start—and stay—laughing:

+ Have a lot of cushions in the room; they can be fun to play with.

+ If you find yourself not laughing, fake it a little. Start saying, "Ha! Ha! Ha!" or something silly like that. You will undoubtedly find yourself bursting into genuine waves of laughter in relatively short order. If you are still not laughing at this point, keep a smile on your face, keep yourself in an amused feeling and wait for the next wave of laughter. It will come.

✦ Make a tape of people laughing or order my laughter tape (see page 194) that you can play to help keep the laughter going.

✦ Do this meditation with a group. Just hearing other people laugh can grease the wheels. If doing this with a group, refrain from talking. Gibberish and sounds are fine, just not words that make sense to the rational mind. You might try sitting back to back with someone, or touch hands or feet. This keeps both of you connected with laughter's infectious vibration. Don't be surprised if you end up in a laughing heap together on the floor.

Try to resist the temptation to compare yourself with anyone, even yourself. (Your laughter will be different from one day to the next.) Try not to judge yourself for not doing it "right." All this comparison reflects the anxiety of the mind, which always wants to judge and compare and make sure we are coming out on top. The great thing is, there is no right way to laugh.

After a week, you'll find you have shed many layers of tensions and you'll be extremely relaxed. You will also feel energized, full of aliveness and positivity. You will discover a greater awareness about the comedy that life can be and a new sense of humor about yourself.

STAGE TWO: *Crying*

The reason people feel better after crying is that they may be removing, in tears, chemicals that build up during emotional stress. Emotional tears have a chemically different content from irritant-induced tears like the ones that appear when we slice onions. Something unique is happening when we cry emotional tears. When we use the expression "to cry it out," that literally may be true. People do feel better after crying.

—DR. WILLIAM H. FRY II
Crying: The Mystery of Tears

The second week of the Mystic Rose meditation is for crying. For three hours each day, you'll just allow yourself to cry and feel your feelings without talking or analyzing.

Through the crying week, you'll be releasing old wounds and gaining insights and understandings as old memories are allowed to surface. Getting out from under the weight of sorrow that you may have carried around for years can bring deep relaxation.

When I teach this meditation, many men tell me how much they appreciate the chance to relax and be themselves, to show their soft and gentle side. And when men allow themselves to feel, to express tears and sadness and be vulnerable, this promotes healing of issues between men and women. Many couples who go through the process together find it brings greater depth, compassion, and understanding to their relationship. Of course, the crying week is also enormously healing for women.

There's not much mystery about the technique, though keeping the room dark can help you move into your sadness. Sitting or lying down, just close your eyes and move deeply into all the feelings that make you cry. Gently open the dam that's been holding all your pent-up feelings, all your sadness and grief. Just let the tears flow out of you. If you feel blocked or get sleepy after crying for a while, try some gibberish. Get into a fetal position and rock your body back and forth a little. Just let the tears come.

After the three hours of crying, sit silently for fifteen minutes. Just watch whatever is going on inside and outside.

As you do the crying technique, be careful not to fall asleep or daydream or "space out." The mind will try to keep you occupied with other thoughts because it doesn't want to lose control. Remember the mind has learned to control, so letting yourself cry means releasing a lot of old conditioning about controlling yourself and your feelings. This week it's okay to not be okay.

A major key here is acceptance. One of the ways we create psychological pain is by fighting what is happening when the feelings are uncomfortable. The fight creates more pain. If we can find the courage to accept, the pain will heal itself more quickly than if we fight it.

Don't force the tears. Just allow them to happen. Tears are mysterious—they come on their own. Some days of the crying week you might cry in a flood, others more softly and quietly. Some days you might not cry at all. That's fine; just stay present with your feelings.

Until I started doing the Mystic Rose, and experiencing the crying week, I did not fully understand what had been happening to me through all those years of stuffing my feelings.

I was born and raised in London, England. The emotional environment was stiff upper lip, grin and bear it, have a cup of tea, and let's all pretend that everything is fine. The English are masters at repressing emotions and keeping everything "under control." I learned quite early that I had to hide, stuff down, and control my feelings, and so my childhood was spent largely numbed from emotion. I really don't remember expressing my feelings much at all.

When I first tried the Mystic Rose, I didn't cry much. In fact what came up was anger. After the breakthrough of the laughter week, I felt that I had spent enough of my life connected to depression, misery, and suffering. All I could feel was anger, so I used the crying time to get in touch with the pain that was underneath it. Anger, as I discovered, is aggressive pain. By differentiating anger from pain I was then able to understand and heal myself on a much deeper level.

Another time I wasn't particularly aware of pain, only boredom. By probing a bit, I discovered that allowing and accepting the boredom took me into deeper layers of feelings. Staying with the feelings, the dam did eventually burst and tears just flowed out of me. This was the first time I cried with such compassion and acceptance for myself, with such awareness and consciousness that I was healing myself. It was the first time I consciously took responsibility for my painful feelings instead of blaming others for them.

After doing the crying week, my appearance literally changed. I could see my face, my eyes, jaw, neck, and shoulders begin to relax. I looked years younger, healthier, more alive. Instead of hanging on to my sorrows, I found an ability to free myself from the burden of them so that I could open up and allow my soul to sing. This is what the crying week is about—freeing ourselves from the burden of old pain. What has been deemed a weakness is in fact one of the most powerful healing forces on earth.

Both laughter and crying release emotional tension; they are two sides of the same coin, but in the Mystic Rose we start with laughter because it is easier to laugh than to cry. Laughter prepares us to open up; it helps us to move into our hearts so that by day eight we are very ready to cry and to feel. Then, after seven days of crying, we feel cleansed, opened, and deeply relaxed, ready to move into the last stage, where we will integrate the processes of laughing and crying.

STAGE THREE: *The Watcher on the Hills*

This last stage of the Mystic Rose, the Watcher on the Hills, serves as a centering meditation, after all the expression and emotional release. A lot of space has been opened up in you in the past two weeks and you now have an even greater capacity for silence, peace, and spiritual nurturing.

For a total of three hours each day, you will alternate sitting silently, witnessing your thoughts and emotions, as if you are what Osho called "a Watcher on the Hills," with short intervals of gentle dancing. You'll need a comfortable place, loose-fitting clothing, and some of your favorite relaxing, soft dance music.

Choose a quiet place where you'll be comfortable and undisturbed. Sitting either on the floor or in a chair, head and back straight but not rigid, with eyes closed, just breathe naturally and relax. Become a witness to whatever is passing by, a "Watcher on the Hills." It doesn't matter what you're watching; it's the process that's the meditation. Try not to become identified with or lost in any particular thoughts or feelings; just watch, witness.

After sitting for forty-five minutes, put on some gentle music and dance softly for fifteen minutes. Allow your body to find its own movement. Be gentle with yourself but don't get lost in the music. You want to stay aware and continue watching. After fifteen minutes, you'll return to sitting. Repeat this forty-five-minute sitting/fifteen-minute dancing cycle twice more for a total of three hours.

The Watcher on the Hills is about awareness, focus, and staying awake. You don't *do* anything; you just relax, but this is an alert relaxedness. In this week, you are practicing disidentification—the capacity to step back and watch. Let yourself be with the moment and watch whatever is happening. Thoughts, feelings, body movements, outside noises—allow them all to be a part of your awareness without judgment.

We are not used to this doing nothing. This meditation is a way to help us move from doing to being, from out to in. If you become aware that you've spaced out or gotten lost in your thoughts, simply come back to the present moment and go back to watching. No judgments, no comparisons, no goal, simply be.

Any time you feel the need to change position, do it with awareness so that it becomes a part of the meditation. Say to yourself, for example, "right now I am moving my leg." Then simply watch the thoughts as they pass by, the emotions as they come and go. The mind and the ego will want to make it complicated, but it is not. It is very simple. Watch, without judgement, and with total acceptance of what is.

And let the mind pass by.

You can imagine yourself as if one would sit high up on a mountain top, watching life pass by with no attachment or involvement.

The first time I did the "Watcher on the Hills" was also the first time that I sat in a silent meditation for any length of time. Believe me, the thought of being just me with my mind for three hours a day for a week was not an exciting prospect. But as is so often the case, the reality was a pleasant surprise. I actually found it rather easy to sit and just absorb the changes and insights I'd had over the previous two weeks. The point here is not to close off the mind—in fact my mind was very active—but to learn to watch it and to develop the awareness that we are not, in fact, the mind. We can simply observe what goes on in the mind as if from a distance.

Once we reach that place of watcher or witness or observer, we suddenly see ourselves with more clarity and objectivity. We can look at all the dramas in our lives with perspective and compassion.

Sometimes I think of this as gardening, as taking care of the flowers (intuition and inner wisdom) in our inner gardens. In order to nurture the seedlings we must be watchful of weeds (negative, fearful thoughts and judgments) so that the flowers can come to full bloom. We must also be watchful of intruders who might crush and destroy the flowers. When the gardener is home (watching, observing, but not judging) the flowers are safe and can blossom, offering their beauty and fragrance to whoever passes by.

Becoming a Watcher on the Hills frees us from the supremacy of the mind. It allows our inner wisdom full expression, which then creates the very opening we need for the insight and perspective to create our lives just the way we want them to be.

Part Three

REFINING
THE GOLD

Creating Your
Own Practice

For those of you who would like some suggestions for getting started with your own practice, this chapter should give you some ideas to work with.

I have included a Beginner's Plan, which would be a great introduction for anyone seeking the benefits of meditation. After a month, beginners could then move on to the Mid-Level Plan or begin to experiment with other techniques. The Mid-Level Plan is also a good plan for someone resuming a meditation practice. The Advanced Plan is not only for those of you with previous meditation experience but for anyone who wants to jump in and start with the longer techniques. The Dynamic Plan, for example, is also great for beginners. The Love/Intimacy/Compassion Plan was designed especially for those of you who are feeling disconnected, either from your partner or from your own heart.

To get the best results, set some time aside *every day* and stick with a given practice for *one month*. After one month, you may choose to stay with the same techniques or substitute one of them for another similar technique. Remember that you are discovering methods that you enjoy, suit your lifestyle, and work for you. We are all different. What works for your friend or spouse, for example, might not work for you. Never compare. Stay with yourself and build your own unique practice.

Don't force it. Meditation should not be a forced effort or it will be doomed from the very beginning. Forcing creates a subtle tension, a contraction in the body. Some of us are body-oriented, some heart-oriented, and some intellect-oriented. The methods in this book can be used by all three types. Just choose a method that you enjoy and go into it as deeply as possible. If you enjoy a method it means it fits with you, that there is a subtle harmony between you and it. You will be much more likely to stick with your meditation practice if you find a practice *you like.*

Experiment with different techniques. Once you have made the decision within yourself to bring more awareness into your life, start experimenting with the different techniques. Meditation techniques are a set of keys, not a series of answers. Try one and see if it fits. You will know when a key fits because you will enjoy doing that meditation. Give each new technique at least one month to see if you like it. Let joy be the criterion. We have to begin somewhere. It may be a false beginning, but through the groping around, the door can be found. So begin somewhere, anywhere. It doesn't matter. As the ancient Chinese proverb says, "A journey of a thousand miles begins with but a single step." If you wait for the right beginning, then you will never begin at all.

A Beginner's Plan
(Suggested time: 5–10 minutes a day)
Remember, anyone can start a meditation practice; no special skills are required, just your willingness to do it.

1. Breathe (page 30)
2. Walk in the Park (page 130)

Enhance this at the weekend with: Try Sauntering (page 52).

A Mid-Level Plan
(Suggested time: 10–45 minutes a day)
Try each of these for five to ten minutes:

1. Enjoy Yourself! (page 62)
2. Just Sit There (page 130)
3. Walk in the Park (page 130)

Enhance this at the weekend with: Preparing Food (page 136).

An Advanced Plan
This plan is for anyone, beginner or longtime meditator, willing to put more time and commitment in each day. You will get more deeply rooted results from the longer meditations.

1. Early A.M. Dynamic (page 44) (do not eat before this meditation)
2. Eating Meditation (page 97)
3. Gibberish (page 41): ten minutes gibberish, ten minutes sitting silently (you might like to use my *Gibberish Meditation* tape. See page 194).

Dealing with Stress: Short Plan

Some of you are looking to meditation to help with stress. Perhaps you've heard that meditation is good for your physical health, particularly for your heart. That is absolutely true. These techniques are some of the best de-stressors I know. Try the Short Plan any time you're under pressure and have a few minutes to spare. If your stress is particularly acute and/or you can find the time for the Longer Plan, try it. I'm sure you'll find that it gives you deeper and more lasting results.

1. A.M. Stand on the Earth (page 31)
2. Bring Your Awareness to Your Body (Simple Reminders, page 51)
3. Jogging (page 35)

Dealing with Stress: Longer Plan

1. A.M. Working Out at the Gym (page 35)
2. Eating with Awareness (page 129)
3. Shaking (page 39)

A Morning Routine

This might suit those of you who do shift work or those of you willing to get up thirty minutes earlier. In the mornings we are at our most fresh and receptive to the meditative state. Beginning with a meditation will transform the quality of your whole day.

1. Ten-Minute Sitting (page 32)
2. Just Ordinary Tea (page 96)

Love/Intimacy/Compassion Plan

If you are having problems with your relationship, or just want more love and intimacy in your life, try these techniques. You also might want to try my *Opening to Love Meditation* CD (see page 194). They are simple yet powerful resources to bring you more of what you want. Love begins with loving yourself so give yourself a treat and bring more love into your life.

1. Feeling More Loving (page 144)
2. Couples Meditation #1 (page 145)
3. Cherish Yourself, Cherish Others (page 122)

Dealing with Emotions Plan (Including Anger/Frustration)

One of the most effective ways to release pent-up emotions is the Gibberish technique. Wherever you can find a suitable place, let it all out. One of my clients used to do this in her car at lunchtime. You will be amazed how relaxed and calm you feel afterward. When the "charge" has been released, you can then approach situations with greater clarity of mind.

1. Gibberish (page 41): ten minutes gibberish, ten minutes silent sitting

You might like to use my *Gibberish Meditation* tape (see page 194 for ordering information).

Finding Yourself Plan

Think of an issue that touches a nerve for you that you would like to bring more awareness to for one week. It might be a problem at work or with family or friends. Meditation can help bring clarity; creative solutions can arise. After one week, you might want to continue for one more week, or for one month until you feel complete with the exercise.

1. Sit Silently and Wait (page 96)

A Travel Plan

When we travel we leave our normal routines—of diet, exercise, etc.—behind. Here are some suggestions to help with the stress of travel. You can do these anywhere, at any time of day or night.

Sometimes, for example, when I'm in a crowded, chaotic airport waiting for a delayed flight (don't you just feel that frustration rising?), I listen to music under headphones, close my eyes, feel my feet on the ground, and breathe. When a situation is not in our control, instead of tensing up in anger, we can respond to it in a creative way for ourselves.

1. Relax the Breathing
2. Listen to Music (page 130) (Use headphones. Music recommendations on page 193. My *Guided Relaxation* with music on page 194.)
3. Eating with Awareness (page 129)

Preparing for an Interview

Some of my clients have asked me what could help them before an interview. I particularly recommend this technique to help you feel calm, grounded, and self-confident. (On page 194 is listed my tape of this method: *Transforming Tensions Meditation*.) You might even remember during the interview to keep your legs uncrossed, feel your feet on the ground, and breathe. The more relaxed the body is, the more relaxed you will be.

1. Transforming Fear into Love (page 179)

Before a Meeting

A short meditation technique before a meeting can have a powerful effect on enhancing composure while negotiating, facilitate better communication and teamwork, and encourage new ways of seeing and doing projects.

1. Ten-Minute Sitting (page 32)

Whichever techniques you choose, relax and enjoy them. Meditation is not some serious or forbidding task; it is something to be enjoyed. The point is not to achieve anything but simply to discover yourself. Try to stay fully present. Anytime you are fully present, you are meditating.

Remember, too, that meditation and relaxation build on themselves. It's only difficult in the beginning. Once you start paying attention to the meditative core of energy that is already within you, it will grow. Eventually you will reach that point of "effortless effort" as they describe it in the Zen tradition, where you are making an effort but everything flows so easily that your effort feels effortless.

Questions and Answers

Now that you've had a chance to try on some meditation practices, you will undoubtedly have some questions. In this section, you'll find a chapter of answers to the questions most frequently asked by my students—everything from questions about postures and whether or not you should close your eyes to how to stop the mind or how to deal with distractions. I hope you find answers to your own questions here.

Of course, answering our questions doesn't resolve all the difficulties and obstacles that occur when we embark on an inward path. In the next chapter we'll take a look at some of the most common obstacles people encounter as they move inward. I want to encourage you to persevere. We all have fears to face—no one gets a free ride!—but in my experience it does get easier as you continue.

Q. Do I have to shut my eyes?

No, you don't have to. You can meditate with your eyes open. I do recommend that you keep your eyes shut, however, especially if you're a beginner, because there's a lot to distract you when your eyes are open. Also, when we close the eyes, a certain relaxation happens in the body. All the energy that was going out through the eyes can now go inward, to recharge the batteries, to regenerate us.

If you find it difficult to keep your eyes closed, try wearing a blindfold that fits comfortably and see if this helps. After a while your body will get used to the idea of closing the eyes for meditation.

Q. Can I do more than one type of meditation in one day?

Sure. Choose techniques you enjoy. If you choose short ones, you can do several different ones in a day.

Q. Do I have to sit to meditate?

No. As you've seen, there are many meditation techniques that do not require sitting. You can find many to choose from in this book.

Q. How can I stop my mind?

Don't even try. Simply relax the body and watch the mind. Become a witness to it. Let the thoughts pass by. Over time you will learn to become less identified, less in the grip of the incessant chatter of the mind.

Q. How can I control the thoughts in my mind?

Don't try to control them. You will just generate a fight and even more problems will arise. It is perfectly natural for the mind to have thoughts—good, bad, all kinds of thoughts. The mind is an outlet for our creativity. The key is to become a witness to the mind, to relax the body and watch the thoughts pass by with no judgment. Slowly, over time, you will acquire the knack of knowing when to pay attention to the thoughts, for example when you are having new ideas about expanding your business, and when to let them pass by, such as when you are practicing a silent sitting meditation.

Q. I just can't sit still to meditate. What should I do?

Many people have this problem. It's difficult to sit still when the body is full of mental, emotional, or physical tension. Try the Moving meditations in Part 2, Chapter 1. These are designed to release stresses from the body/mind *first* so that it is then easier to sit in silence.

Q. What should I do with all the uncomfortable feelings that come up when I meditate?

Try to accept them. Just allow them to be there, with no judgment, just compassion for yourself. If you try to get rid of them, repress them, fight them, they will grow and create even more trouble. Simply relax, watch, and accept. In their own time they will pass.

Q. In the Stop technique I noticed I was not present in my body but very concerned with what else was going on in the room. How can I stop that?

You don't have to stop it, just bring awareness to what is with total acceptance and compassion for yourself. Practicing a meditation technique is not about being "the perfect meditator" and "getting it right" but awareness of what is, then acceptance.

Q. Am I supposed to concentrate on something?

Concentration or any kind of forcing of the mind to focus on one particular thing can create a subtle tension in the body. The harder you try the less will be achieved. Simply relax the body, bring your awareness to the breathing, and watch whatever is happening. The more relaxed you are, the easier it is to meditate.

Always begin with bringing awareness to the body. Begin where you are, in the body. Check that your body is comfortable. Any time you might need to change position, do it with awareness so that it becomes a part of the meditation. Then simply watch your thoughts as they pass by, the emotions as they come and go. The mind and the ego will want to make it complicated, but it is not. It is very simple.

Q. Is there any particular time of day that is better for meditation?

In the morning we are more receptive, fresh, and in touch with our inner wisdom and clarity, our hearts. After a night's sleep we tend to be more relaxed. It is easier to meditate in the morning.

However, you might prefer to do some of the active meditations, for example the shaking, dancing, or gibberish, at the end of the day to get rid of the day's tensions from the body/mind. So there is also value in meditating at the end of the day, too.

Q. I don't really understand how meditation can help me when I have a very busy stressful job with many deadlines.

If you create a regular practice, whether it's five or ten minutes a day to do perhaps a simple breathing technique, slowly, over time the quality of meditation and relaxation will become an undercurrent to your workday. You may not be able to get rid of the stress of your job, but you will be far better equipped to handle it.

Q. I don't have *time* to meditate or relax. How can I fit this in?

Do you have thirty seconds? Take thirty seconds right now to be with yourself, to connect with yourself on the inside. And do it totally. You see, it's the quality of the time you spend that's important, not the quantity. Better to spend thirty seconds a day, and be total with it, than an hour where you're struggling against the time and distracted and your heart isn't in it.

Start with one of the short meditations in Chapter 1 or Chapter 5. Remember, take it easy, take it slow, one simple step at a time.

Q. This thirty minutes seemed like ten. Is that normal? This ten minutes seemed like thirty. Is that normal?

Yes, both are normal. When the mind is very busy, time seems to drag; when the mind is more quiet, time seems to go quickly. As you meditate, you will probably have both experiences. Try to stop yourself from judging and comparing those experiences. One isn't better than the other. Simply accept whatever is happening: enjoyable, unenjoyable, busy mind, quiet mind.

This ability to witness whatever is happening with no judgment will bring you in touch with your inner haven of peace, calm, and serenity. Remember there is no right or wrong with meditation, there is simply what is.

Overcoming Difficulties You May Encounter

You gain strength, courage and confidence by every experience in which you really stop to look fear in the face. . . . You must do the thing you cannot do.

—ELEANOR ROOSEVELT

Being able to meditate doesn't require any special degrees or skills or attributes. It's something anyone can learn to do. And yet many people say they cannot do it. Why not? What happens when we close our eyes and go inside? Why don't we want to stay in there?

Perhaps we don't like what we find—the insanity of the mind, the fears and anxieties it creates. We don't want to be alone with uncomfortable emotions: pain, jealousy, anger, despair, hopelessness. We don't know what to do with them. So we keep ourselves occupied with the outside, with work, with any kind of busyness and decide to ignore them, perhaps hoping they'll go away.

As you gradually become more centered in yourself as, slowly, the subtle joy and peace that meditation brings pervade your being, the obstacles seem less overwhelming. And, of course, you can always return to the Laughing meditation to remind you of your sense of humor.

Fear

Which of you, by worrying, can add one span to his lifetime?

—ALAN WATTS

It is often fear that keeps us from meditating.

What are we so afraid of? Of being ourselves, of discovering who we are. There is, of course, a vast difference between true fear and the kaleidoscope of anxieties that choke so many people today. True fear is a survival signal that sounds in the presence of danger. It is not voluntary; it will come and get our attention when needed. All animals know this. Anxiety, on the other hand, is the fear that we manufacture in the mind. It is this anxiety that keeps many of us from meditating.

In his Pulitzer Prize—winning book *Denial of Death* Ernest Becker describes humans as "hyper-anxious animal[s] who constantly invent reasons for anxiety, even when there are none." Unwarranted fear has assumed a power over us that it holds over no other creature on earth. Unlike true fear, unwarranted fear is rarely logical. An awareness practice can help you tell the difference between the two.

It can help you reverse the process of contracting in fear; it can help you become aware of your fears. By seeing them for what they are and standing with them, we find that they no longer have to control us. This takes courage. I think we often mistake courage for fearlessness; it is not that at all. Courage allows us to stand in our fear without becoming controlled by it.

I don't mean to suggest that this is a simple question. One of my clients had the courage to admit to me that she was afraid of meditation. One would expect to be afraid of encountering a lion or a tiger in one's backyard, but encountering ourselves? Perhaps that is an even greater fear. I suggested that she first just allow the fear to be there.

Admitting to it out loud was a great first step. Perhaps we have learned it is cowardly or weak to say we are afraid, but fear is a natural part of life; everyone feels it at one time or another.

Then I suggested she start with some of the simple techniques like the ones you encountered in Part 2, Chapter 1 of this book. I also suggested that laughing and accessing feelings of love can help dispel fear and asked her to think about how she could bring more of those into her life.

It took her some time to feel self-confident. But by accepting her fear, by allowing it to be there, she saw how it would disappear of its own accord whenever she was fully in the present moment. She saw how in the face of happiness, fear simply dissolves.

The meditations I have personally found the most powerful in lessening the controlling grip of fears in my mind are Osho Dynamic (see page 44), the Mystic Rose (see page 149), Gibberish (see page 41), the Laughter (see page 63), and the Dancing (see page 37). Through constantly doing these techniques, and others, over the last twenty years, I am now able to hear more clearly the wisdom of my body and heart and to act from an integrated place rather than from the controlling mind alone.

Meditation helps us move from the mind, where fear, suspicion, anxiety live, to the heart, where we find courage, trust, love, compassion, humor, and friendliness. Not that we want to erase the mind. We need it. But only when it's balanced by the heart can it shower forth its best stuff—a wealth of creativity, of positive thoughts and ideas.

We all need to take reasonable precautions in our lives to reduce risk and simultaneously reduce anxiety. The awareness cultivated through meditation helps us see hazards in the storm clouds only where they truly exist and guides us to live life more fully in the clear skies between them.

Techniques for
Moving Through Fear

If you find yourself often gripped with anxiety, try this gentle technique: Every night before you go to sleep repeat "yes, yes" and get in tune with it, sway with it, let it come all over your being from your toes to your head. Let it penetrate you. Repeat "yes, yes, yes." Let it be your prayer for ten minutes at night and then go to sleep.

Then early in the morning when you wake up, the first thing to do is repeat "yes" for at least three minutes. Get into the feel of it; experience it to your very bones.

During the day, if at any time you start feeling worried, anxious, depressed, negative, start saying "yes, yes, yes." If you can say it out loud, do so. Otherwise say it silently to yourself. And try to feel it; feel your body resonating with the words "yes, yes, yes."

Another technique that can help is to name your fears. Say them out loud, especially if you can tell a friend, someone who loves you. Their power over you will diminish.

If you feel afraid about doing something, ask yourself, what is the fear? What am I afraid of? This is a powerful first step to lessen the grip of the fear so you can take action and move forward. See if you can take action despite your fears. Walk into them. As Eleanor Roosevelt says, "do the thing you cannot do."

Technique for Transforming Fear into Love

I learned this technique from Osho and many people find it very helpful. Sit in a chair or whatever posture is comfortable for you. Fold your hands together in your lap with the right hand underneath the left hand and with the thumbs joining each other. This is important because the right hand is joined with the left brain, and fear comes from the left brain. The left hand is joined with the right brain and courage comes from that side. So this brings the energy into a healthy relationship and will help to bring you to balance.

Now close your eyes, become aware of your breathing—the in and out of the breath. Allow your jaw to drop down a little and relax so you can start breathing through the mouth. When you breathe through the mouth it goes directly to the chest. This will help to create a new pattern for the breathing system and will help you form a new habit.

Sit silently, doing nothing, for forty minutes. By and by reach to sixty minutes. And do this every day. If you cannot do this for forty minutes, then start with ten and gradually build it up. (You might find my CD *Transforming Tensions Meditation* helpful. See page 194.) But do it every day. After a few weeks you will notice a difference. More courage, less fear.

Awkward Positions

Another prime obstacle that keeps people from meditating has to do with the traditional postures. Perhaps meditation conjures up an image of sitting uncomfortably in a lotus position, chanting mantras for hours on end. Not very appealing? I agree. That's why I don't meditate that way and that's why so many of the meditations in this book involve no sitting. I hope you've seen by now that meditation is a quality that can be brought to any activity: dancing or speaking gibberish or laughing or jogging. If you haven't gotten rid of that mental picture of the yogi in the lotus position by now, get up and try some of the moving meditations in Part 2, Chapter 1. Find a technique that works for you.

Thoughts About Getting Nowhere

The problem is not the thought that you are not getting anywhere. *The problem is that we identify with these thoughts and think that this is reality.* We think that this means we really aren't getting anywhere. But *the mind knows nothing about meditation.* Meditation is beyond the mind. *The truth about our meditation is felt by us as an experience.* It is not a thought. And *our hearts will always tell us the truth about our meditation.* So beware of thoughts from the mind telling you anything at all about your meditation practice, good or bad. The good will just inflate the ego, and the bad will try to seduce you away from your practice. Simply watch both players in the tennis match, disidentified, with no judgment.

Shoulds and Oughts

This is a good time to remember that we are not trying to get anywhere in meditation. Simply be in the present moment with everything that it contains. The mind will try to create problems, telling us we should be more this or more that. It can be very cunning and catch us unawares. So here's another opportunity to watch the mind and its tricks. Just come back to the present moment, with a total acceptance of what is. This is the only place to be.

The Chattering Mind

The mind is a difficulty: It keeps up its incessant chatter and will try to dissuade you from meditation. It likes to be in control. You don't need to drag your mind around with you twenty-four hours a day. You can learn to use it when you have plans to make, or you're shopping, or you're figuring out your latest software acquisition. But when you're relaxing, taking a walk, doing your laundry, for example, you can learn to dis-identify from the mind and let thoughts pass by. Think of the mind as a chair. When you need to sit down, you use the chair. Otherwise you don't use it. You don't drag it around with you everywhere you go.

Nature is on our side here. Our natural master is not the mind; it is the heart. The mind is a very good and obedient servant. This is its rightful place. With your continuing practice of meditation, sooner or later the mind is bound to find its right place.

The Spiritual Ego

Prepare for the attacks of the ego, thinking that you have "arrived," that you know it all. The mind can be very cunning and is always greedy. Spiritual seeking can suffer from the same ego attachment that compels one to seek wealth or power. So beware and watch and keep your connection to your heart.

What Stops Us Continuing?

A little bit of meditation and you start to feel better. Things look rosier, the trees are greener, there is love in your life, so you stop. You think because things are going well, you can stop meditating. But the energy you have generated for your meditation will disappear if it is not regenerated on a regular basis, and then you will be back in the same old turmoil. And perhaps worse, because your disappointment that it didn't last will be added to the mix. Once the decision has been made, commit yourself to it. Accept the challenge of this beautiful journey, of your inner search, and don't stop until you have reached to your innermost core. Then the quality of meditation will be with you as a constant companion.

Expecting and Waiting

There is a difference between expecting and just waiting. In expectation there is a desire, a clear-cut goal. This expectation will block your progress. When you are just waiting, and you don't know for what, you open to trust—a trust that something so beautiful can happen that your mind cannot even conceive of it. A miracle. There's an openness about waiting, a sense of total receptivity, an innocence. If you can do this, the wonderful flowering of meditation will come upon you when you least expect it.

Groping in the Dark

Groping in the dark is part of the journey. It can be extremely helpful to become aware of your hindrances and obstacles: Why are you not always in meditation? Where has the growth been stopped? Where have you been crippled? The very groping will liberate you from darkness. Knowing where your hindrances lie brings you to your own truth, and truth is freedom. Understand this freedom.

Reframe the way you see "difficulties." Learn from them. Remember that a priceless pearl begins as an irritation to an oyster.

Why Are You Meditating?

You will be faced with this question sooner or later.

Be honest with yourself. Are you meditating because it is fashionable, because everyone is doing it? If this is your motivation, you will be disappointed. Then it is not about meditation but about not wanting to be left out.

The desire to meditate has to come from a deep-rooted place in yourself. Because you want to know who you are, because something needs to change, because the way you are going through life just isn't working. You sense the need for something more, something more deeply fulfilling than acquiring material possessions, having a great job, looking great.

Superficial motivations will yield superficial results, but if the reason is deeply rooted in your being, and you persevere, despite all the obstacles, despite a lack of reward at the beginning, you will be richly rewarded.

A Few Secrets

I know of no more encouraging fact than the unquestionable ability of man to elevate his life by conscious endeavor.

—HENRY DAVID THOREAU

As Thoreau says, we have this incredible ability to elevate the quality of our lives, so let's use it. Over the course of the book I have given you a wide range of techniques, from thirty-second techniques to some that take three weeks, from simple techniques to longer, more energetic ones. You have also learned how you can incorporate meditation into your daily schedule, into activities you already do, into your work, your relationships, your leisure time. But if I had to summarize the best of what I know about meditation, this list of fifteen secrets would be it. My hope is that they will help you hone in on the gold that is waiting for you.

Practice Every Day

A daily routine can really help develop your hunger for meditation, especially in the beginning. Even if you have just ten minutes a day to start, commit to meditating every day. Most people also find it helpful to meditate at the same time every day. It doesn't matter what time of day you choose; just think about what will work best for you. When you get up in the morning, for instance, your body/mind expects to eat breakfast. It's your habit; it's what you always do. You can make the same habit with meditation.

Remember, however, that no matter how organized or disciplined you are, you cannot control the process of meditation. Make a container for it that allows you to be at ease and to wait and meditation *will* happen.

Create a Special Place

When you want to plant a rose garden, you first prepare the soil. Stones and roots have to be removed. You have to create the right conditions, the right space. You have to protect your space with a fence. All these preparations are needed if you want to cultivate roses. The same is true for meditation.

But what are the right conditions for meditation? What is the right space? It's best to have a special room for meditation. A small corner will do, but set it aside especially for this. The place itself will become meditative because every act creates its own vibration, and every time you meditate that space will absorb those vibrations. On the following day, the vibrations will start falling back on you. They help, they reciprocate, they respond.

If you prefer to be outdoors, you might try meditating under a tree—trees are in constant meditation. Or lie on the ground and look up at the stars. Or sit by the side of a stream, or find a quiet beach or lake. You want to feel the life energy flowing, pulsating, streaming around you. If your only connection to nature is a fire escape or apartment balcony, then make that your meditation space. The right conditions are always available.

You might also want to have a special meditation cushion, stool, or chair. Take the phone off the hook, and disengage yourself. Take your shoes off, and with your shoes, leave behind everything that you are preoccupied with.

Wear a Blindfold

When the eyes relax, the body is better able to relax. That is why we keep our eyes closed for meditation. It makes it easier to go inward. Especially at the beginning, covering your eyes with a blindfold keeps you from having to think about closing your eyes. It removes that one additional stress. Remember, always choose what's easiest.

Be Playful, Enjoy Yourself

A good way to know if a method is working for you is if you're enjoying it. My rule of thumb is this: Practice the techniques you enjoy and enjoy the techniques you practice.

There's no reason to approach meditation as something grim and serious. Have fun with it. Enjoy the comedy, the madness that is released from within you. Enjoy the feeling of being unburdened, refreshed like a child again.

Don't Hide from Yourself

Each of us is born as a seed, waiting to flower and offer our own unique beauty to the world. Meditation can help you discover yourself, find the courage to face your fears, and be who you were born to be.

Show Compassion for Yourself

Always keep a positive attitude toward yourself. Meditation is not about being perfect; it's about *being*. Accept yourself the way you are. Never compare. Remember to love and value who *you* are and what you have to offer.

Relax in Your Ordinariness

Try not to strive too hard for some notion of meditation perfection; just allow yourself to be who you are. Meditation is not about remarkable physical feats or instant enlightenment. It is about relaxing into the wonder and enjoyment of the ordinary, the mundane, the very grit that life is made of.

Allow for Spontaneous Happiness

We usually think we need a reason to be joyful: We've bought a new house, we have a new love relationship, our son or daughter has just graduated from college. But these joys are momentary. They are dependent on the outside. When happiness is *caused* by something it will always be momentary, transitory. And after the high, you will often experience a lower low, a deep sadness.

The happiness that comes from meditation is a different kind of happiness altogether: You are suddenly filled with joy for no reason at all and you cannot pinpoint why. If someone were to ask you why you are so happy you would not have a reason. The marvelous thing about this kind of happiness is that it cannot be disturbed. Whatever happens it will continue. This happiness remains, like a thread woven into the fabric of your day. When outer circumstances change but the joy abides, then you know you have found your own inner joy, which no one can take away from you.

Let Your Body Be Your Guide

Meditation shouldn't feel bad. If you find yourself becoming depressed by a silent, sitting meditation, it's time to move your energy. Your body will tell you. If you feel good, go with it, but if a silent, sitting meditation makes you feel worse, try gibberish or running, jogging or whatever physical activity you enjoy. And then try again to sit.

Practice Nondoing

Our culture places so much value on doing, on "getting some-where." It's extremely difficult for most of us to get comfort-able with nondoing. Nondoing teaches us nonattachment to any result other than the sheer joy of being. In this nonat-tached state, you can often tap a rich creative vein and your essential self can become known to you. Any creative person knows this: The tension created by desiring results inhibits the creative process and distorts the ability to see connections clearly. The point is to just let them happen, to let go of desire and let what comes come.

This moment is complete in itself. Nothing else needs to happen.

Deautomatize

If I could share just one secret, this would be it. Bring a medi-tative awareness to everything you do. Whether you're walk-ing, running, brushing your teeth, or taking out the trash, do it mindfully, with awareness. When you listen to someone talking or gossiping, listen attentively, be present. When you look around, look watchfully.

When you deautomatize you can see the wonder that exists all around. The flowers will seem more colorful than they've ever been, the trees greener.

Integrate Meditation into Your Life

We don't separate out breathing from the rest of our lives—in the morning you breathe and then you go to your business and forget breathing—it runs like an undercurrent through all the activities of your day. The same is true of meditation. Whether you are a lawyer in court, an assistant in a store, a reporter on a newspaper, digging a hole in your garden, or driving in traffic, you can do it consciously, with full awareness, bringing the quality of meditation into your whole day.

Meditation can become as natural to you as breathing.

Don't Expect Instant Nirvana

If you expect instant nirvana you will become discouraged, tense, anxious. Have patience. The flowers of meditation do not come on demand. Whatever you are ready for will happen. If nothing is happening, then perhaps you're not ready. Prepare the ground by continuing to meditate and then wait. When the heart and the energy are coordinated, results happen.

Pay Attention

The word "attention" comes from the French word *attendre,* which means "to wait for." Derived also from this is the English word "tend." As we tend to our inner garden, with love, care, and attention, one day the flowers will bloom. Not because we forced or controlled, but because we prepared the soil, planted the seeds, then watched over them. All the tips, techniques, and suggestions in this book are meant to help you

tend your inner garden. If you pay attention, you will start to
see the seeds sprouting, the stalks growing, and one day, suddenly, the flowers bloom, the fruits appear on the tree.

Allow Meditation to Happen

Sitting silently
Doing nothing,
The spring comes
And the grass grows by itself.

This haiku, a Zen poem by the Japanese Zen master Basho,
transmits the very essence of meditation. The first word, sitting,
reminds us that we begin with the body, and as the body
becomes relaxed and restful, the mind will become more
silent. You are not doing anything, simply delighting in rest.
There is no hurry, no worry, expecting nothing, simply waiting. The spring comes, not because we willed it, but because in
the natural rhythm of things, it will come; it is bound to. Once
you have understood this, then you know the greatest secret—
that there are things that you cannot do, but can only allow to
happen.

RECOMMENDED CDS AND TAPES

The CDs mentioned throughout the book can be ordered from the following sources:

For a selection of relaxing music, my CDs, and the Osho meditation CDs:
   Prabhu Music
   To order: 1-877-466-2583
   Web site: www.prabhumusic.com

Other recommended music:
   Shastro and Nadama:
   Tantric Heart: Music for Lovers, Shastro
   Healing Touch, Nadama
   ZeNotes, Shastro and Nadama
   Web site: www.malimba.com
   Telephone: 800-334-1179

Miten and Deva Premal:
Web site: www.MitenDevaPremal.com

Anugama:
Web site: www.openskymusic.com

Sambodhi Prem:
Web site: www.globalsuitcase.com

If you're interested in finding out more about Osho's meditations, or to order his books or the music tapes and CDs that
were created to accompany his meditation techniques, visit
www.osho.com. This is a comprehensive Web site in different
languages featuring Osho's meditations, books, tapes, and selec-
tions from Osho's talks. Of Osho's many wonderful books, the
ones I would particularly recommend for meditation are *The
Book of Secrets* and *Meditation: The First and Last Freedom.*

For more information about my consulting, trainings, classes,
workshops, and private sessions, please see my Web site:
www.pragito.com or e-mail me at pragito@pragito.com.

My "Lunchtime Enlightenment" Meditation CD Series
with Music is also available through my Web site. This series
currently includes the following CDs, each of which may be
purchased separately. I have created these CDs as companions
to the book, not readings *of* the book. I hope you enjoy them.

1. *Guided Relaxation / Transforming Tensions Meditation*
2. *Opening to Love*
3. *Wisdom of the Body*
4. *Laughter and Tears*
5. *Insomnia*
6. *Witnessing the Mind*
7. *Gibberish*